The

CASHMERE

New Zealand Immigration Ship 1851–1863

By Belinda Lansley

*Ancestral Journeys
of New Zealand
Series*

Without the help of the following people this book would not have been possible. Special thanks to:

Maritime Museum of New Zealand, for photos of the *Cashmere* model
Andrea King, for Thomas Stokes bio
Marolyn Diver, for help on the book cover

Published by Rock Your Boat Publishing

Harewood, Christchurch
www.greatgrandmaswickerbasket.blogspot.co.nz

Original text © Belinda Lansley 2016
Images © named individuals, institutions
All rights reserved
ISBN 978-0-473-27398-9

Cover Design by Belinda Lansley

Dedicated to our ancestors who came to New Zealand

Belinda Lansley

Great great great granddaughter of William Pearce,

Schoolmaster on the Cashmere, 1859.

Contents

Introduction	7
The Ship	9
The Voyages of the *Cashmere*	25
Cashmere Passengers	93
Passenger Lists	109
References	*125*

Introduction

The *Cashmere* is one of my ancestral ships. It transported my great great great grandfather William Pearce, barrister's clerk, to Lyttelton in 1859. On researching this book, I had an amazing find! I discovered William was schoolmaster on board the ship – a new genealogical discovery for me. On arrival in New Zealand, William became an Inspector of Nuisances for the Christchurch City Council. This position was something like the first dog control officer / environmental officer / traffic warden! He did everything from instructing people to remove dead bloated horses from empty lots, to ordering sewage to be disposed of correctly. He also enforced hackney carriage rules. He was bitten by dogs, assaulted by irate cab drivers and everything else you can think of. He was probably very disliked by many people in Christchurch. So this book is for him!

All sources are referenced carefully at the back of this book. Some sources may have errors. Often in the past people exaggerated or made incorrect entries in the records. Advertisements for ships often made a ship sound better than it really was in order to gain passengers, just as advertisements operate these days. So I have worked with what was available and hope this written record is as accurate as possible.

If anyone has further information on the ship *Cashmere* including ship diaries, family letters or comments in their family histories about the journey that they are willing to share, please contact me so it can be added to any future updated editions.

Belinda Lansley

belinda.lansley@yahoo.co.nz

The Ship

Construction of the Ship

The *Cashmere* was an English ship, built in 1850 in Sunderland, England. It weighed 574 tons using old measurements and 640 tons under the new system with a weight of burden of 1000 tons.[1] The weight of burden was a good guide as to the maximum cargo allowed on board that would make the journey economic, as well as making sure the weight was not exceeded which could cause the ship to sink while at sea.[2] The ship was sheathed in yellow metal in 1850 and repeatedly re-sheathed in felt and yellow metal over the years. It measured 130 feet long, 30.5 feet breadth, 20 feet depth. From the tonnage alone, we can tell that it was a smaller clipper ship than many that came in later years to New Zealand. Some larger ships weighed well over 1000 tons.

The Macky family who came out on the ship in 1854 commissioned a amazing model of the *Cashmere*. The craftsman who made it copied the Blackwall Frigate style of the original ship. A Blackwall Frigate had a single gallery and was superficially similar to a frigate of the British Navy. It was made to scale with the same length, breadth and depth. Pictures of the model are in the following pages. She had the typical black and white banding down the side and the name was painted in gold on the ornate stern, "*Cashmere* – London." The model flies the "red ensign" a bright red flag with a small union jack in the corner and the figurehead is a man in a blue naval style jacket. She was certainly a fine ship. The model is now held in the New Zealand Maritime Museum in Auckland and is on display if anyone wishes to view it in the flesh.

Internal plans of the ship also survived over 160 years and are held at the Alexander Turnbull Library. They can be found on pages 14-15.

The *Cashmere* was not a true clipper ship like many of the immigrant ships. Clipper ships had three masts and square sails and it was this combination that made them so fast and popular in the 19th century.[2] The Cashmere, being a Blackwall Frigate would have been a bit slower and this is shown in the average journey times to New Zealand which never went below 100 days and could be up to four months at sea or more. Most clippers had average journeys of about 3 months except in very adverse conditions where the journey could be prolonged.

The Ship

Model of the Cashmere, *New Zealand Maritime Museum Collection*

Model of the Cashmere, *New Zealand Maritime Museum Collection*

Model of the Cashmere, *New Zealand Maritime Museum Collection*

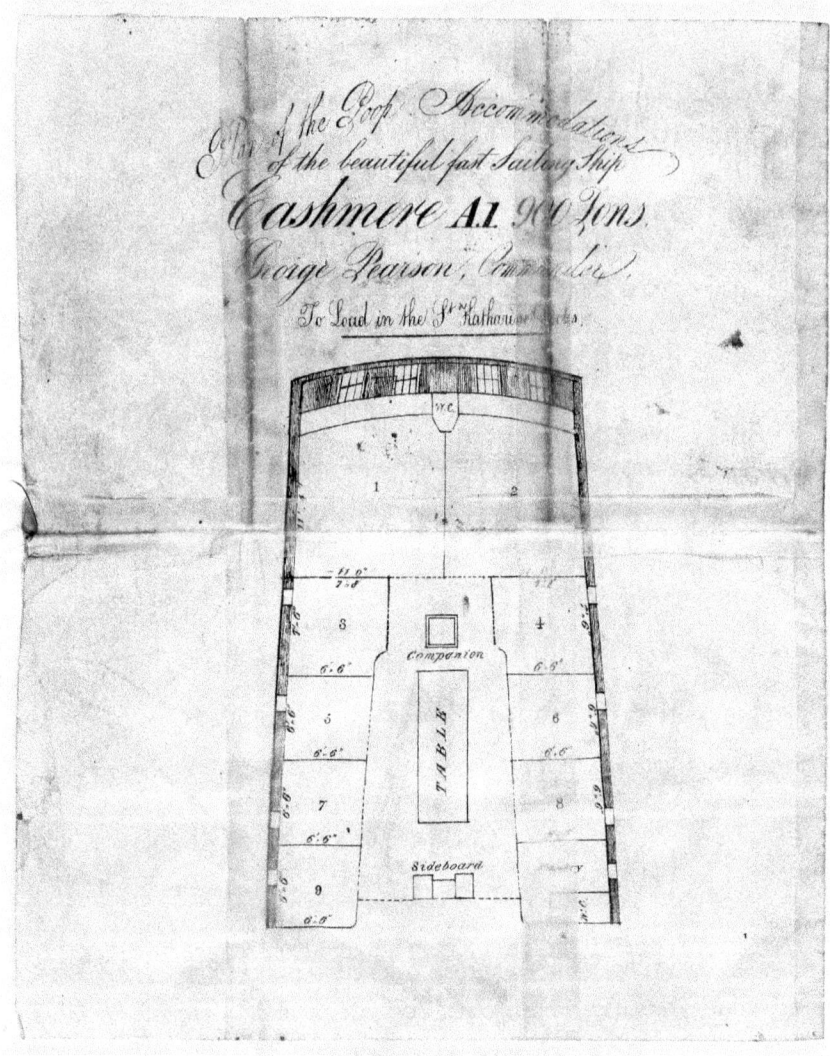

Plan of the Cashmere. The above plan shows some poop accommodation. The next page shows that the between decks were used for cabin accommodation as well as steerage. Cabin measurements are included. (Alexander Turnbull Library, Wellington, NZ, William Kirk, MS-Papers-7207-01-PLAN)

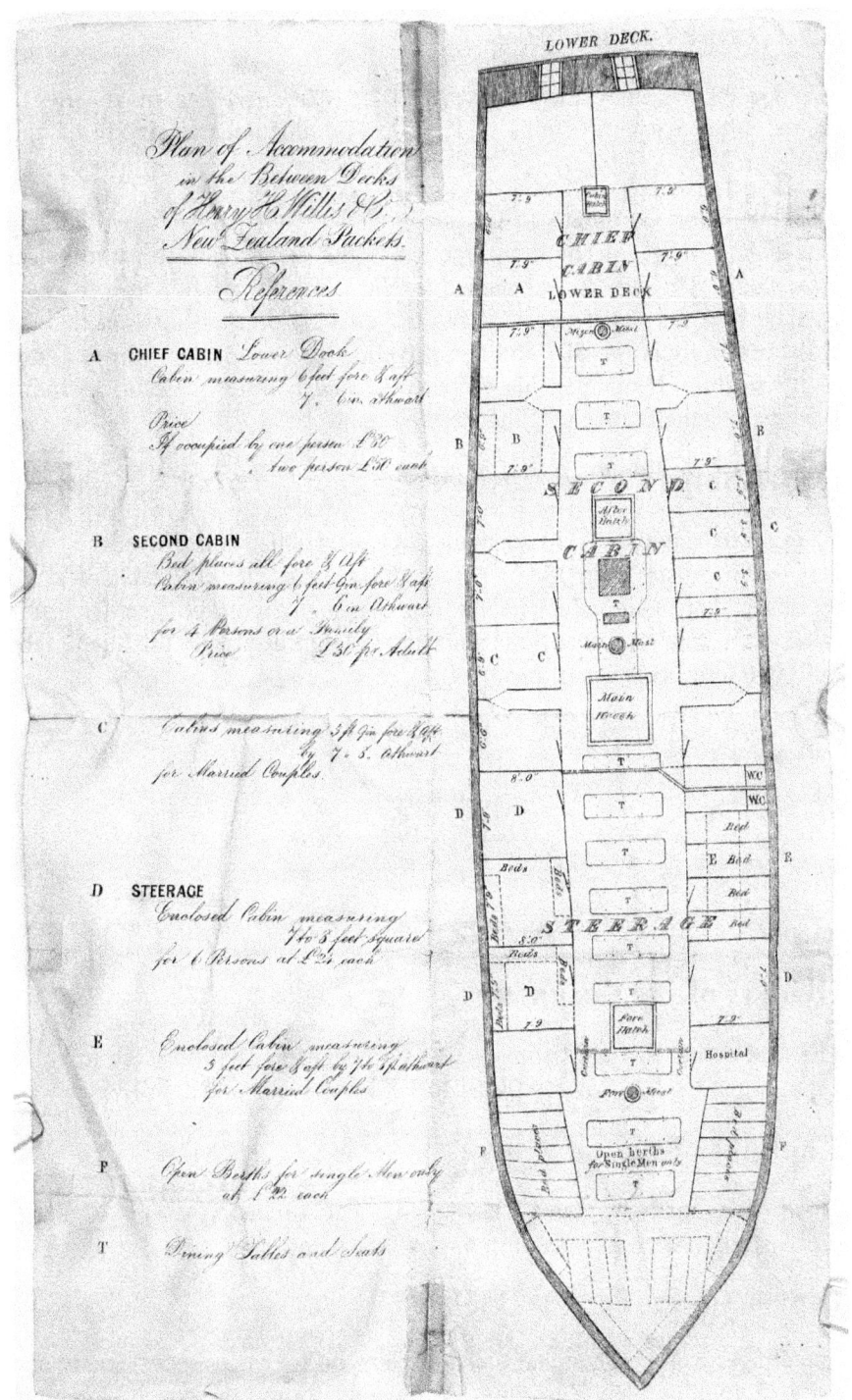

The Name *Cashmere*

We don't know why the ship was named *Cashmere* but maybe it was named after Kashmir, India. There is no documented proof of this however.

The suburb of Cashmere in Christchurch was not named after the ship *Cashmere*. It was a common practice in the early years to name places after ships. The suburb was named by Sir John Cracroft Wilson who took up land near the Port Hills in 1854 after arriving on the ship *Akbar*. John was born in India in 1808 and had travelled to New Zealand for the good of his health. He named his property *Cashmere* after Kashmir in India. Cashmere is the British spelling for the region.[3]

Other Ships Called *Cashmere*

There was another ship named *Cashmere* that was wrecked near Newcastle, Australia in 1882. Also a ship named *City of Cashmere* was a regular visitor to New Zealand and was eventually wrecked near Timaru in 1882. It is important that these ships are not confused with the Sunderland built 640 ton *Cashmere* of this book.

"City of Cashmere" wrecked near Timaru in 1882

Owners of the *Cashmere*

The first owner of the *Cashmere* was C. Tebbut in 1850 through to about 1860. Then Park & Co. from 1861 to 1863 and Ivens & Co. in 1864.

Captains of the *Cashmere*

There were many captains that sailed the *Cashmere* to New Zealand, successfully bringing loads of immigrants to a new land.

Captain George Pearson (1851-1857)

Captain Pearson commanded the *Cashmere* on four trips to Auckland and one to Lyttelton, New Zealand. He eventually ran the Naval Hotel and the Family Hotel, both in Auckland. He died on 4 April 1886. After his death, his wife and children moved to Sydney, N.S.W.[4]

Captain John Byron (1859-1860)

Captain Byron was master of the *Cashmere* in 1859 when the ship arrived at Lyttelton. He was charged with neglecting to deliver letters that were on the ship on arrival at Lyttelton . They had been loaded at Gravesend by the broker's clerk. Captain Byron didn't know of the letters at all and the receipt stated there were only two packages in the bag.

Captain Petherbridge (1860-1862)

Captain Petherbridge took the *Cashmere* to Port Chalmers and Lyttelton in 1861 and Auckland in 1862. He sailed other ships such as the *Maori*, *Napier* and *Countess of Kintore*. Captain Petherbridge sailed it for five years. He brought the ship *Maori* to Nelson when first launched in 1851 and then again in 1853. He did the trip in 88 days which was incredibly fast! After being commander of the *Cashmere*, then took over the *Napier* in 1863 and did a passage of 83 days to Nelson, the fastest to that date!

Captain Petherbridge shipped birds to the Colony on the *Napier* in 1863. These included seventy pairs of partridges, skylarks, blackbirds, thrushes, starlings and goldfinches. On the *Countess of Kintore* in 1870 he brought our 50 rooks which were landed at Auckland all alive and healthy. The *Countess of Kintore* traded mostly to Auckland, landing hundreds of passengers and her saloon was always filled with passengers on the way home.[5]

He became Superintendent of the Colony for Shaw, Savill and Co. and then returned to England permanently. Before leaving he was presented with a purse of sovereigns by the merchants of Canterbury, to purchase a service of plate in England.[6]

Captain Barnett (1863)

Captain Barnett commanded the *Cashmere* on a trip to Nelson in 1863. He was previously in charge of the ship *Cresswell*.[7] He was a well-known figure in the Nelson area and was praised for his high level of seamanship.

Two Competing Companies

The *Cashmere* was chartered as a packet ship by two competing companies at different times in its career. A packet ship was originally used for shipping post office mail to the colonies and other places around the world but this meaning was eventually extended to include passengers as well as mail.[8] Shaw, Savill & Co. and Willis, Gann & Co. advertised regularly in English newspapers, competing with each other for passengers.

Willis, Gann & Co. were first known as Henry H. Willis & Co. but then changed to Arthur Willis, Gann & Co. in 1856.[9] In 1858 Robert Shaw and Walter Savill left Willis, Gann & Co., one of the leading companies sailing immigrants to New Zealand in the 1850s, and formed their own company called Shaw, Savill & Co. Shaw, Savill & Co. were to become one of the most well-known and respected shipbrokers in the trade. The *Lord Ashley* was Shaw, Savill & Co.'s first ship to sail from London, on 28 May 1858. By 1865 the company had fifteen ship journeys running on the New Zealand service and in 1866 this increased to 68 ship voyages.[10]

The *Cashmere* was run by Henry H. Willis for the first 5 journeys. This company was then renamed as Arthur, Willis, Gann & Co. who advertised the *Cashmere* for the 1859 and 1860 journeys. The 1861 and 1863 journeys were with Shaw, Savill & Co. who took over this famous immigrant ship from the other company, probably because it was starting to bow out of the New Zealand trade.

In 1854 the provincial governments became responsible for immigration. The Province of Canterbury had the largest immigration scheme of all the provinces, bringing in almost a fifth of all immigrants between 1858 and 1870. Two thirds of all passengers arriving in Canterbury were assisted; generally, half of their fare was paid by the Provincial Government.[11] The price for a steerage ticket was anywhere from £8 to £20, but on average most fares were around £13. In 1863 rival company Shaw, Savill & Co. secured the contract for carrying emigrants to Otago, the fares being £12 from Glasgow and £13 10s from London.[12] They had the majority of the market at this time. The charges for passengers on board the *Cashmere* on the Lyttelton journeys were as follows:

	1855	1859
Single man or woman	£21	£16 10s
Couple	£42	£33
Child	£10 10s	£8 5s
Infant	free	free

The rates for cabin passengers on the *Cashmere* in 1854 under Henry H. Willis & Co. were as follows:[13]

Chief Lower cabin measuring 7ft 6in by 6in cost £80 for one person, or £50 each for two people.

A second cabin measuring 6ft 9in by 7ft 6in for four people or a family this cost £30 per adult. Also available were second cabins for married couples measuring 3ft 9in by 7ft 8in.

Enclosed Steerage cabins measured 7 to 8ft square were for 6 persons at £24 each. There were also cabins for married couples measuring 3ft by 7ft 8in.

In enclosed steerage there were also open berths for single men only at £22 each.

The average annual wage for a housemaid in 1850's-1860's was from £11-£14[14] therefore the full cost of the journey was a full years wage. The average annual wage for a farm labourer in England and Wales in 1860 was £30 2s 4p[15], so the full cost of the journey was over a third of their annual wage. We can now see that travel to New Zealand was expensive and what a struggle it was to raise even half the fare. They often had help from family and friends already in the colony and of course the Provincial Government would assist by paying part of the fare.

Life on Board a Clipper Ship

The Henry H. Willis & Co. chart from the 1854 period, on the following page, shows the food allocated to the different classes of passengers on the *Cashmere*.[13]

In later years the second cabin and steerage passengers received lime juice to keep away the scurvy. Records show that there were usually, fowl in coups to produce eggs and meat, and sometimes larger animals for fresh meat.

Water was stored in barrels and became stale and often grew algae or had vermin fall in and die. Food was stored in lidded barrels but if someone left the lid off they could often become contaminated with rat and mice droppings. The bad hygiene often led to dysentery, cholera and many deaths on board. Flour often had weevils.

SCALE OF DIETRY FOR EACH ADULT PASSENGER PER WEEK[13]

Articles	Chief Cabin	Second Cabin	Steerage	Articles	Chief Cabin	Second Cabin	Steerage
Preserved meats	1 ½ lb.	1 ½ lb.	½ lb.	Tea	4 oz.	2 ½ oz.	2 oz.
Preserved Salmon	½ lb.			Coffee	4 oz.	2 ½ oz.	2 oz.
Soup and Bouilli	1 lb.	½ lb.	½ lb.	Butter	½ lb.	½ lb.	½ lb.
Ham	1 lb.	½ lb.		Cheese	½ lb.	¼ lb.	
Tripe	½ lb.			Currants or	¼ lb.	¼ lb.	
Fish	½ lb.	¼ lb.	¼ lb.	Raisins, Muscatel or	¼ lb.		
Salt Beef	½ lb.	1 lb.	1 lb.	Raisins, Valentia	½ lb.	½ lb.	½ lb.
Salt Pork	1 lb.	1 ½ lb.	1 lb.	Suet	½ lb.	6 oz.	4 oz.
Biscuit	3 lbs.	4 ¼ lbs.	3 ¼ lbs.	Preserved Carrots	½ lb.		
Flour	4 ½ lbs.	4 ½ lbs.	3 ½ lbs.	Pickles	¼ pint	¼ pint	¼ pint
Rice	1 lb.	1 lb.	½ lb.	Vinegar	¼ pint	¼ pint	¼ pint
Barley	¼ lb.	½ lb.	½ lb.	Mustard	½ oz.	½ oz.	½ oz.
Peas	½ pint	1 pint	½ pint	Pepper	½ oz.	¼ oz.	¼ oz.
Oatmeal	½ pint	½ pint	1 pint	Salt	2 oz.	2 oz.	2 oz.
Preserved Milk	½ pint			Potatoes, fresh or	3 ½ lbs..	3 ½ lbs.	3 ½ lbs.
Sugar	1 ¼ lb.	1 lb.	¾ lb.	Preserved ditto	½ lb.	½ lb.	½ lb.
Treacle		¼ lb.	¼ lb.	Water	28 qts.	21 qts.	21 qts.

Illness was rife on some journeys, especially when steerage passengers were confined below decks during massive storms in the Southern Ocean. The ships were cleaned with vinegar and chloride of lime to remove vomit and make things smell better, while precious water was kept for drinking.

Toileting on ships was not pleasant. Often pieces of rag, soaked in vinegar, were hung on the back of the toilet door. These were used to wipe with and were shared over and over often leading to dysentery! The sewage was often flushed into the bilge with buckets of water until emptied at port. The bilge was below steerage so the stench was not pleasant. People would be horrified these days but back then hygiene was generally not understood.[16]

Married couples' accommodation in steerage: bunks to the left and right; central table; light from the uncovered hatch. (London Illustrated News, 13 April 1844)

The sleeping arrangements were bunk beds for steerage with single women and single men having their own areas. Families often became separated as, most of the time, children over the age of 12 were transferred to the single men's or single women's quarters. Bedding was aired in fine weather but often became soaked if water was coming into the ship and this led to influenza and pneumonia outbreaks.[16]

Some ships were better managed than others. The *Cashmere* was generally well managed with no majorly tragic journeys to New Zealand and the expected levels of mortality.

On the more positive side, a ship journey such as this would have been one of life's biggest adventures for the emigrants. They would see and experience things they never dreamed of, including strange sea creatures, new constellations in the skies and a sea voyage which most would never repeat again in their lifetime, culminating in a strange new land at the final port. At night the passengers entertained each other with music, lectures of the new country and games, made new friends and contacts and looked forward to a brighter future in their new country.

Crew of a Clipper Ship

The average crew of a clipper ship without migrants was about 17, including the Captain, First Mate (or Chief Officer), Second Mate, Midshipman (Apprentice Officer), Ship's Carpenter, Boatswain, 9-10 ordinary seamen and the Cabin Boy who was used for mundane duties. There were usually two cooks. The Passenger's Cook who made food for the steerage passengers and the Ship's Cook for the cabin passengers and crew, who catered for their more refined tastes.

The crew numbers became closer to 40 when emigrants were on board, with additional crew being the Ship's Surgeon and Constable to keep the passenger welfare attended to. A Schoolmaster was on board, to teach the children and a Matron to separate the single woman from the single men. Sometimes there was a Minister on board. There were usually several Stewards who looked after the Cabin Passengers. Some people took up a job on board to get free passage out.[17] The Matron was often a woman looking to emigrate who took on the job in exchange for free passage.

Wages for the crew were on average £7 per month on the way to New Zealand, with good food and comfortable accommodation, but up to a £100 wage for the home journey, to ensure crew stuck with the ship and didn't desert once in New Zealand. Even with the better wage, desertions were common.[17]

Crew of the Amazon, 1886 (State Library Queensland)

The Demise of the *Cashmere*

The *Cashmere*, ship of 640 tons, didn't have an exciting ending, crashing on rocks or sinking dramatically. She was sold in 1869 to a timber merchant, Messrs Carswell & Davis, of Glasgow, for £2,800.[18] Her fate after sale is likely scrap wood. She was probably sold to carpenters and builders to be turned into all manner of things. However we can't say for sure how she finally ended her life. The *Cashmere* disappeared from Lloyd's Register and was no longer the amazing ship she used to be, worn out from all her journeys around the world.

Example of a boat, heeled over in the shipbreakers yard, (This ship is named The Queen*). (Creative Commons Attribution Licence 3.0)*

The Voyages of the Cashmere

There were nine voyages for the clipper ship *Cashmere* which are summarised in the table below and discussed individually in more detail using diaries, newspaper articles and other official documents.

Date Sailed	Date Arrived	Captain	From	To	Days
16 June 1851	19 October 1851	Pearson	**London**	Auckland	125
22 October 1852	9 May 1853	Pearson	**London/ Plymouth**	Auckland	102 from final departure from Plymouth
	6 July 1853			New Plymouth	
20 April 1854	6 August 1854	Pearson	**London**	New Plymouth	118
	21 August 1854			Auckland	
2 July 1855	23 October 1855	Pearson	**London**	Lyttelton	101
	22 November 1855			New Plymouth	
19 December 1856	5 April 1857	Pearson	**London**	New Plymouth	116
	14 April 1857			Auckland	
11 June 1859	11 October 1859	Byron	**London**	Lyttelton	105
1 November 1860	9 February 1861	Petherbridge	**London**	Port Chalmers	100
	15 February 1861			Lyttelton	102
15 December 1861	7 April 1862	Petherbridge	**London**	Auckland	113
3 July 1863	14 October 1863	Barnett	**London**	Nelson	103

1851 Voyage to Auckland

16 June 1851 – 19 October 1851

The *Cashmere* left Gravesend on 16 June 1851 with Captain Pearson in charge and 103 passengers. Passenger Albin Martin wrote a diary while on board.[19]

He comments that he boarded the ship on 13 June, so had plenty of time to get his cabin in order. There was a delay on the ship sailing due to a "child having an eruption on its face." This had to be checked in case it was smallpox with the ship finally sailing three days later. A pilot took charge of the ship until Deal. They were apparently well paid me, receiving as much as £15 for two days work. The first week the ship was tacking back and forth due to a head wind which added to their sea sickness. When tacking the ship would have been leaning on its side. This often made it difficult to walk or do anything. Even writing a diary would have been hard.

"The night after our pilot left us, it being vey dark and misty, we ran into a French fishing-smack; two of the men got on board our ship: one of them, the captain of the smack, bewailed the supposed loss of his boat, and abused our sailors in no very delicate French, but which, as they did not understand it, had very little effect. I happened to be awake at the time the accident occurred, and jumped up, I must own, rather frightened; the passengers thought we had come on a rock, and some of them were much bewildered." Eventually the men went back to their boat.

On board the ship was a lot of livestock for the journey ahead. This included thirty dozen fowls, one dozen sheep, thirty pigs, and a cow for milk. Ten of the fowls died within the first week as they were "crowded to death." The remaining birds would have been a lot happier that their numbers had been reduced. One sheep and three pigs were killed every fortnight.

". . . the first porker was put to death in a most barbarous manner; the man who came on board as butcher did not understand his calling. On taking the pig out of his pen, a string was tied to his leg; he immediately made a bolt, and darted into the lap of seven young ladies, who were sitting reading novels and knitting opposite the cuddy door; the surgeon's bulldog, thinking the pig very unpolite, joined in the fray; the squeaking of the pig, the barking of the dog, the screams of the seven sisters, and the laughter of the sailors, rendered the scene most amusing to the lookers-on."

They saw a few birds, sharks and dolphins but none had been killed yet. As a form of entertainment, bottles were thrown out from the stern to be shot at but they were very hard to hit.

On 29 June Albin wrote that the weather had been cold and that all his children had been very ill, except Walter. Albin himself was very sick when the sea became rough. They watched a vessel come in sight and the captain signal it with flags. There were two clergymen on board and the next day, Sunday, they had a church service in the morning. In the afternoon a Northcountryman, an Independent minister, preached for a good hour in a terribly strong accent and with a lot of repetition and this was very hard to listen too!

The Captain was apparently inclined to stop at Madeira (maybe he liked the place) but told the passengers there wasn't time to stop anywhere.

On 2 July Albin commented that "Every thing on board goes on in the same dull way;" The seasickness was not allowing Albin to read or pay attention to anything. Most of the passengers were feeling the same way. He said that they had the following schedule of eating which made them feel they were living only to eat.

7.30am Children's breakfast

9am Adults' breakfast

1pm Children's dinner and Adults' lunch

4pm Adults' dinner

6pm Children's tea

7pm Adults' tea

After all the food people went on deck. Those who could sing did so, and those who could tell good stories had lots of listeners!

On 3 July at long. 16°25' W lat. 32°58' N they viewed the outline of the Island of Porto Santo. The ship was averaging 180 miles per day for the past three days. The sailors had little to do but scrub the decks at this stage and the captain had them all in good order. The first and second mates were described by Albin as "good officers."

On 4 July they passed and only just viewed the Island of Palma, one of the Canary Islands; a place of excellent wines and a safe harbour. The passengers were starting to get over the sea sickness finally. Twenty six people including cabin passengers and officers sat down to dinner every day. The cook was very good and Albin was hopeful that the sheep and pigs would hold out until the end of the journey.

7 July and Albin commented on the monotony and how the colour of the sea had not changed for several days. There was a school on board, held by Mr Dudley, a clergyman. Mergie and Fanny, Albin's children, attended this and enjoyed it, with improvements noticeable. The air was getting hot and the cabins very stuffy or "close." Albin was in a cabin at the stern which was great for him. Others had some below. If they left the windows closed they were stifled, if they opened them they risked being drenched by a wave. This meant many passengers were hanging out their clothes to dry on this day.

On 12 July they missed Cape de Verde as the captain was not that close to these islands and the air was thick. There was rough weather and more sea sickness. They had tropical rain and tubs and baths were brought out. Mr. Brodie began his wash. Several other people then joined in. "The passengers came on deck in every possible variety of oilskin and India-rubber dresses; many of them with very little dress on at all. The scene was quite new to most of us, and was as great a change as could have happened." The temperature reached 80 degrees Fahrenheit and they saw several flying fish. One jumped on board! The sailors had him for breakfast as they were very good to eat.

"I hope the passengers will keep good friends with each other. A voyage of this sort brings out all selfish and unreasonable qualities in great force. One person thinks he has not his allowance of water; those who sit at the bottom of the table think all the worst things are put at their end, and that we at the top get the best dishes. Our captain is most judicious, we cannot be too thankful in having him for our master; if we were left to our own devices, our provisions would, the best of them, be gone before the end of the voyage, and the passengers altogether by the ears."

Sunday 13 July the ship was becalmed. There was a heavy sea and the ship seemed to be going round and round. It was like a seesaw on board. A ship came close enough to them for the Captains to speak by speaking trumpet to each other. The ship was Dutch and was from Batavia bound for Amsterdam. Later in the night ther rain came down in torrents and the ship pitched about. "the noises were beyond description." And people couldn't get any sleep. The rudder made a terrible noise in rough weather, through vibrations. "This, with the trampling of the sailors over head, the rush of the water at the stern (for we sleep with both windows open), the uneasy position of all sorts of things in the cabin, which keep knocking each other about, the nerves must be in a very quiescent state to enable one to get any sleep under such circumstances. I have not mentioned the chance of one of the six children adding its mite to the disturbance."

19 July – for the whole week the ship had adverse winds. At one point a French boat came close and some young adventurous spirits went over in the hope of buying some luxuries (French ships often had them) but came back with just some brandy and anchovies which were sent as a present from the Captain. There was nothing to buy.

22 July they were detained and couldn't seem to reach the equator having had either calms or adverse winds.

26 July at 3pm they crossed the line finally! "The old customs the sailors used to have in crossing the line are now done away with, and they are

much "more honoured in the breach than in the observance" the men have to content themselves with a few bottles of rum; our ship is on the temperance plan, and it is much the best; the sailors are well-behaved, and the captain acts with great kindness towards them, but keeps the most strict discipline."

30 July they were making 150 miles per day which was not fast, but better than before. The boat was often lying on its side and would occasionally give a "great lurch" which was not pleasant for the passengers.

Albin wrote about his perceptions of a sea voyage: "The getting up of a morning is the worst part of the day; it requires considerable effort to get to the washing stand, and when there to maintain a footing. How it is possible for any one to like a sea voyage, I cannot think; one cannot eat, drink, or walk but under great difficulties; then there is the being in prison with the chance of being drowned; other evils may fall to our lot, such as an ill-tempered or injudicious captain, disagreeable fellow passengers, bad provisions, and perhaps but little of them; the last evils we are at present free from, the former cannot be avoided."

On 2 August to about the 6 August the ship was making a bad course and they were lucky if they were doing 3 miles per hour. The sunsets had been very beautiful but there was nothing else of interest to write about.. There had been some disagreements in the cuddy but Captain Pearson had the final say and he had good management of the ship and was kind hearted. The other passengers had no disagreements so the cuddy passengers were not setting a good example. "People situated as we are have not much else to do but to eat and drink."

On 6 August they saw a little English brig of 170 tons called the British Empire. The Captain came on board (which is common when ships are becalmed). They were headed for Montevideo. A number of letters were sent by this brig to Montevideo for forwarding to England. The weather was getting colder and jackets were out. It was hard to write in a journal as "one is so distracted by the cries of the children; ten or a dozen persons are discussing different subjects at the cuddy table, where I am now writing; there is a great trampling and noise overhead on the deck, and the intermediates at the cuddy door are amusing themselves by laughing, singing, whistling, and talking; sometimes the lurch of the ship comes which obliges one to hold on to the table with both hands. We have plenty of time and opportunity of studying each others' characters; I do not think any one of us is likely to set the Thames on fire; we are rather an odd mixture of individuals, but I must wait till the end of the voyage before making any more remarks. Few seem to know what they are going to do on arriving at New Zealand; each is curious to find out the plans and prospects of his neighbour."

On Saturday 9 August they saw the island and ports of Trinidada. Albin did a sketch of the Martin Bass rocks. They saw some nautili. The looked like piece of pink ribbon floating about. The weather was fine and the sunset that night magnificent.

14 August and they passed from summer to winter in a matter of days. It rained in torrents this day and the wind was a gale. The sailors however said it was "only a little fresh." The captain ordered all the sails in except two as the ship was straining. ". . . it was curious to see the men on the yards, clustering like bees; I thought they were in a dangerous situation enough as it was; how they manage it in a heavy gale I cannot tell…"

If you tried to stand up you were in danger of being thrown by the movement of the ship. The next day was fine and the light and shade on the water was very beautiful. Cape Pigeons were around the ship and they were not easily caught with a hook, the bait being a piece of fat. Stray albatrosses were also seen but not in great numbers yet.

18 August and Albin commented that the next land to be seen was Tristan da Cunha. "This place had some soldiers on it during the time Buonaparte was at St. Helena; when they were removed, one of them named Glass, having a liking for the island, remained there with his family, others joined him, and they number now more than 100 people. Glass is called governor, and they live very contentedly; a clergyman has gone out to them; ships call for potatoes, sheep and fowls, and give them in return tea, sugar, and clothes; our captain will stay a day at the island if possible, but if there is a rough sea, I would not give much for our chance."

In the bad weather the rudder had been shaking violently and the vibration was felt through the ship. No one wanted to sit at the cuddy table while a large ham was on it, in case it launched itself at a person during the lurching of the ship.

20 August and they saw Tristan da Cunha but they didn't go on shore as it was too rough and were very disappointed. Albin talked about his baby boy who nearly got his fingers cut off with a pair of scissors when trying to grab them off his sister Emily about four or five weeks earlier. One finger had come away to the first joint, that day, so that hopefully the rest of the finger could now be saved. Albin was glad it wasn't worse.

There had been more grumpy passengers and complaints about the steward who had a "very unpleasing" manner..

On 21 August Albin was offered a shot with Mr Read's gun and brought down an undertaker bird, a kind of ugly black gull.

On 25 August some more complaints were made and passengers were constantly finding fault. The captain spoke his mind in the cuddy. Albin named the passengers as Mr and Mrs B. Mrs B had given herself "airs of exclusiveness" and Mr. B. had behaved with "great rudeness and incivility." Albin's wife Jemima had no complaints but Miss Goldborough had, making the journey more unpleasant than it needed to be.

On 1 September they were 300 miles off the Cape of Good Hope. Albin said that it was so cold that Mergie, his daughter, and himself had chilblains on their fingers. A gale came up on the 28th. Albin was putting down the leadlights that protect their stern windows, on the Captains request, when there was a great lurch of the ship. Everything was moving to and fro including a large set of drawers. Albin comments, "I had never been in a gale at sea before, and was much gratified at witnessing one of the grandest sights I had ever seen. There was a great deal of phosphoric light on the water, and as the waves rose and broke they appeared like sheets of white flame, innumerable sparks of fire glistened in the track of our vessel, the night was very dark, the deck very slippery from the spray, the wind was so furious that I was obliged to hold on with both hands to the ropes;" No one could sleep that night.

A couple of nights later a huge wave broke over the ship and surged into the cuddy cabins as the door was left open, then proceeded to soak the passengers below and all their bedding. One of the boats was nearly knocked off and four bundles of hay were lost over the side. The boat however was travelling fast at about 200 miles per day.

On 5 September they had a quiet night and the gentlemen were now back on speaking terms. Not the ladies however. Baby's finger was healing and the children all had good health. Walter, Albin's son, cried all night when he first came on the ship, causing much nuisance to everyone. He was now a favourite on the ship. Another son, Albinus took after his father and looked very pale and thin. The ship movement was making him feel sick all the time.

On 9th September the storms still continued. People were falling on the slippery deck, including the cook who injured his shoulder. He made a good pork pie. Albin commented that the children thought the lurching was good fun, but it was not so much for the adults.

On 12 September the weather was still bad. They had seen two waterspouts in the distance, about four miles off. The water was whirling and twisting as it was sucked up from the sea. The night before there was a play acted out by some of the passengers called "Turning the Tables" and the Captain allowed the cuddy passengers to have some supper and a few bottles of wine. Supper is usually not allowed on board ship. "All the sailing qualities of our ship have been lost by the misfortunes of the rudder; she goes very fast, and with all her canvas on, it would take a first-rates ship to beat the *Cashmere*; but, in a heavy sea, most of the sails have to be taken in, for if not, the rudder shakes in a most frightful manner."

On Wednesday 17 September Albin wrote about more bad weather on Saturday night: "The roaring of the wind as it rushed amongst the masts and rigging was terrific; it seemed like some demon determined to gain the mastery over our ship, and at one time it kept everything still, the waves were subdued, and the *Cashmere* was as quiet as when in the docks. We were all glad when the morning came. One cannot help thinking now and then that there are only two inches of plank between us and those tempestuous elements."

On Friday 19 September they passed the island of St Paul's. It had a "fine outline" with the rocks seeming "very bold and grand" The island did not produce anything. The rough weather had helped them to travel very fast and they were making 200 miles per day..

On 24 September the weather was much better, but Albin was concerned that the rudder was shaking much more than it should. There was no remedy but taking in sail.

On 26 September the rough times were forgotten and they were sailing quite smoothly. They were off the coast of Australia (called New Holland). The sailors were starting to clean up the ship so that they "cut a good figure" as they arrived at Auckland.

Albin said "The *Cashmere* is a smart looking vessel; some persons find fault and say she is built too slight, and that she will not stand many voyages; it is possible they may not know much about the matter; passengers are generally fond of finding out the imperfections of their ship. I know nothing of these things, but in justice to the *Cashmere*, I must say she is a very comfortable vessel, a fast sailor, and she seems very water-tight. I never see the men at the pumps; I believe, however, that they are used once a week.."

On 2 October it was calm and Albin says "Our vessel reminds me of Coleridge's idea, "a painted ship upon a painted sea." The air was clear and the skies beautiful. Several large birds were shot to the excitement of the passengers, but Albin saw it as cruel, the birds having their wing broken by the ball and then flying away injured and being pecked at by their companions and pecking themselves.

On 10 October they passed within a few miles of Low Head, a little village with a church and a lighthouse at the entrance to Port Dalrymple, Tasmania. A pilot came out to see them and ask if his services were needed but they weren't. They learnt the news that gold had been discovered at Port Philip "in much more abundance than it had ever been found in California." Men from the neighbouring places were going for the gold. "The news turned the heads of the crew and the plans of many of the passengers will, I have no doubt, be greatly altered." Albin only believed part of the stories as he thought they were third or fourth hand! "The pilot's boat was rowed by six convicts. I never saw rogue more plainly stamped on six men's' faces in my life. If they left their country for their country's good, they most certainly left it for their own; they earn ten shillings per week, get lots of the best food to eat and drink, and are living in the finest climate in the world. This was their own account. "

Low Head Lighthouse which the passengers of the Cashmere *viewed in 1851*

The breeze sprung up and the ship started moving in the correct direction. Mountains, hills, rocks and islands disappeared from sight. They went through the Bass Straits and at 10pm there was land close on each side. It was "rather nervous work." There was a lot of noise later at night and the sailors were getting more canvas on, meaning they were safe and out of the tight spot.

11 October and that week had been the most exciting of the voyage. They had a delay getting through Bass strait, tacking back and forth. The only consolation was the beautiful scenery. They saw the snow-tipped mountains of Van Diemen's Land (Tasmania) and the lesser mountains,

covered with trees. Albin sung the praises of Tasmania! They caught some fish and sharks. Albin helped capture the first shark but firing a shot though its head from down below. They were then able to haul the dead animal up on deck. They also got four sacks of potatoes while in the Straits which were a wonderful treat.

On 17 October land was sighted again, New Zealand! The land didn't look as good as Van Diemen's land but the fact it was a convict settlement meant Albin wouldn't go there. He had heard that you couldn't go out at night there for the chance of getting knocked on the head or robbed was very high. They could see fires burning on shore at New Zealand. Albin thought they would have been lit by the natives.

On 18 October Albin could see that the country was improving. They were now sailing down the east coast towards Auckland.

They arrived the next day on 19 October at Auckland at about 10pm. They rejoiced as the anchor went down. A lot of people left the ship the next day but the Martin family stayed until 25 October when they found a house in Auckland. Albin wrote a testimony for the captain and there were a couple of arguments against the letter, however most passengers signed it in support of the captain's good work.

The newspapers spoke of similar things to Albin Martin. Especially about the rudder. They stated that after leaving Gravesend the ship had favourable winds but they were quite strong. At Lat. 40°S., Long. 22°E. the *Cashmere* spoke the *Seringapatam* travelling from London to Bombay, 59 days out.

The *Cashmere* would have made the journey out easily in 90 days but there was a defect in the rudder irons. The rudder shook from side to side as there was a problem with the dumb cleat. It caused an "extraordinary motion" that made the ship almost unmanageable. Captain Pearson had to "place her under double-reefed topsails with courses stowed – and that with the wind aft, or on the quarter.- Sometimes she was obliged to be hove-to." The *H.M.S. Calliope* which had also come into Auckland twice, had a similar disorder, so bad that it was like a bird wagging its tail.

The *Cashmere* passed Tristan da Cunha (a remote island in the middle of the Atlantic) and probably would have seen the large cone of Saint Mary's Peak rising up from the middle of the island.

Tristan da Cunha

For the 35 days after passing the island, the average daily run was 190 miles per day. In moderate weather with the wind right aft, she rang easily at 214 miles per day. If the rudder had not been defective she would have run easily at 240 miles per day.

On sighting and passing the Launceston Heads the *Cashmere* was boarded by a shore boat. They recommended the captain go to the diggings as Van Diemen's Land (Tasmania) was emptying and Auckland would be deserted! However they kept going!

The *Cashmere* brought out 103 passengers who were all healthy on arrival. They were all very thankful for the "attentive conduct" of Captain Pearson.

It was commented that the *Cashmere* was "one of the handsomest merchant ships" that had been seen at the Port of Auckland.[20]

ON SALE,

FINE FLOUR (V. D. Land), in 50, 100, and 200 lb. Bags
Rice—Soap—Mould Candles—Bacon Mustard—Pickles—Dried Apples Salt—Tobacco Pipes—Negrohead Tobacco Hops—London Porter—Rocking Chairs.

EX "EMMA,"

Congou Tea in ¼ Chests—Rice Java and Loaf Sugar
No. 2 Manila Cigars.

THOMAS LEWIS.

Queen-street, Oct. 11, 1851.

Daily Southern Cross 14 November 1851

GRAHAM & HENDERSON have just opened, ex "Cashmere," from London, a large assortment of Gentlemen's Ready-made Clothing, as under:—

WAISTCOATS,
Black and Coloured Satin Waistcoats
" Cassimere ditto
" " Embroidered ditto
Coloured Barathea ditto
White Marseilles Quilting ditto
Brown Holland ditto
China Silk ditto
Light fancy Thibet ditto
Dark ditto ditto
A variety of Boys' fancy ditto

TROUSERS.
Superfine Black Cloth Trousers
Light Doeskin and Tweed ditto
Moleskin and Corduroy ditto
Boys' Cloth ditto
" Moleskin and Corduroy ditto
" Cloth Suits

SHIRTS.
Long-cloth Dress Shirts
Fancy Regatta ditto
Scotch Tweed ditto
Blue Serge ditto

Auckland, 31st Oc., 1851.

RECEIVED, EX "CASHMERE," FROM LONDON,

SUPERFINE BLACK CLOTH
Ditto ditto Cassimere
Ditto ditto Doeskin
Coloured Doeskins and Tweeds
Cassinette, Linen, and Cotton Drills
Fine White and Printed Quilting
Valencia Waistcoating
Rich White Silk ditto
" Thibet ditto
" Black Satin ditto

GRAHAM AND HENDERSON.
Auckland, Oct. 31st, 1851.

New Zealander, 5 November 1851

[Advertisement]
TO CAPTAIN GEORGE PEARSON,
Commanding the ship 'Cashmere.'

Sir,—We the undersigned, Passengers on board the ship *Cashmere*, having by the blessing of Divine Providence arrived safely in the Harbour of Auckland, take this opportunity, before we separate, of returning you our most sincere thanks, for the uniform kindness, impartial attention, and watchful care with which you have acted, during a four months' voyage, to every person under your charge. The duties of the master of a passenger ship, numbering 103 individuals, are most responsible; they are arduous, difficult, and sometimes unpleasant to perform. We found, that whilst you insisted on having order and good conduct on board, you were always most anxious to promote the happiness, comfort, and amusement of your passengers. Your kindness to us will live long in our recollections; and you may feel assured, that to whatever part of the world your duties may call you, our best wishes will attend you:

W. C. Dudley, M A., clerk,
Thomas Hamer, Independent Minister,
A'bin Martin,
R. L. Brown,
Conrad Reed,
Mrs. Smythies,
Mrs. Martin,
Mr. Ely,
Mrs. Bouike,
Mrs. Hutchinson,
Mrs. Hamer,
Miss Hamer,
Miss Goldsbrough,
Mrs. Bromley,
Miss Tiddy,
Miss Macintosh,
Catherine Conway,
Mary Conway,
Mrs. Ford,
Miss Ford,
The Misses Runciman,
Mrs. Smith,
Jessie Hamilton,
The Misses Cuttriss,
Mrs. Wethered,
Mrs Henderson,
Henry Smythies,
Walter Brodie,
Colin Campbell,
John Graham,
Loftus M yle,
C. Cuttriss,
C. B. Cuttriss,
Thomas Cuttriss,
David Henderson,
John Sanders,
Henry Bromley,
Samuel Ford,
George Runciman,
James Hamilton,
John Williams,
John Mitchell,
Henry Smith,
Thomas Doyle,
Walter Runciman,
James Francis.

To the Rev Charles Dudley and other Passengers per the 'Cashmere.'

The perusal of your kind and complimentary Letter has afforded me sincere gratification. That I have been enabled to render your voyage happy and comfortable, I cannot but attribute mainly to your own endeavours to make the tedium of a sea voyage pass pleasantly away.

That I should bestow "uniform kindness, impartial attention, and watchful care" upon you all, was but my duty; that I have accomplished this in such a manner as not only to please you, but draw forth the very flattering testimony in my favor which you have addressed me, I cannot but feel gratified in learning.

Wishing you every prosperity in the new land of your adoption, to which it has been my pleasing duty to bring you, believe me to remain,

Yours, &c., &c.,

GEORGE PEARSON.

A Blackwall frigate similar to the Cashmere *(R & H Green Blackwall Frigate – artist Stephen Dadd Skillet)*

Map of the Journey of the *Cashmere*

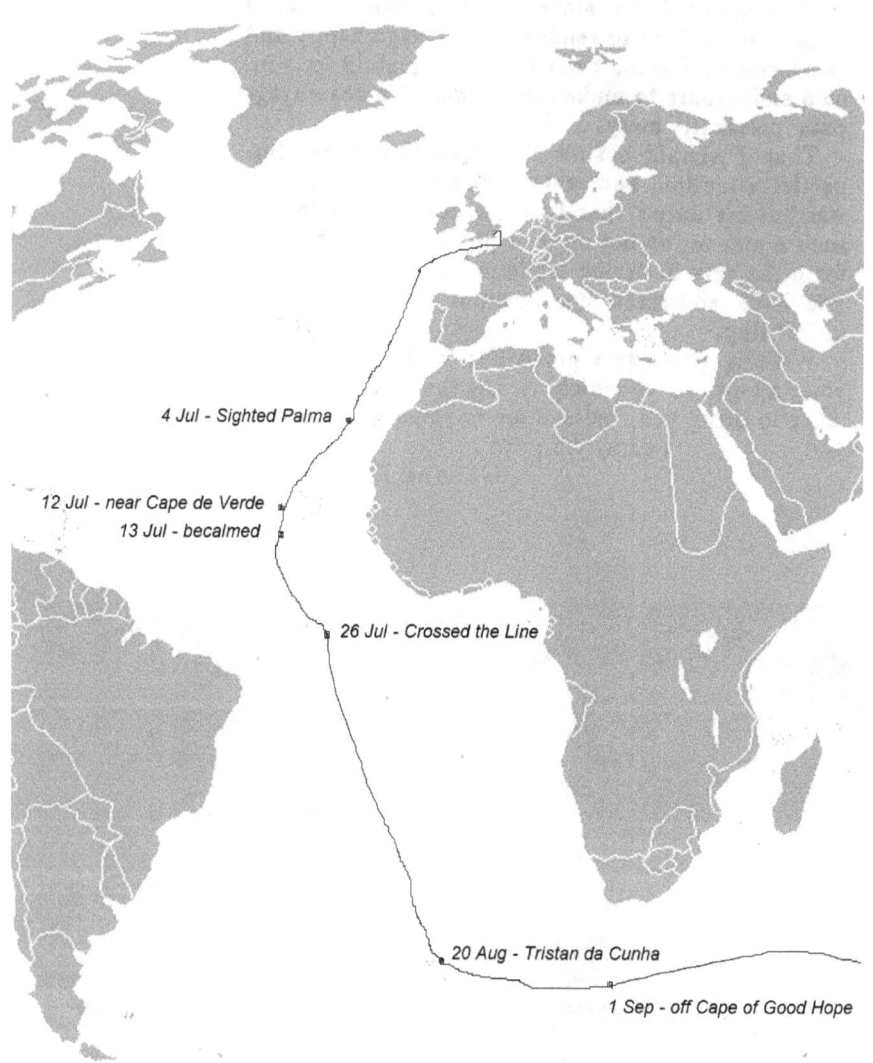

(16 June 1851 – 19 October 1851)

1853 Voyage to Auckland and New Plymouth

22 October 1852 – 9 May and 6 July 1853

This was arguably the worst voyage for the *Cashmere*. The *Cashmere* was described as a "remarkably fine ship." It had a full cargo and 85 passengers.[21]

The ship left Gravesend on 22 October but they were detained in the English Channel until about 14 November. With much difficulty they managed to put into Falmouth at one point, sailing again on Sunday 21 November.[22] After finally getting to sea on 24 November at Latitude 49° 8' N. Longitude 50°42' W she was thrashed about by a strong gale. It did much damage including loss of bulwarks, stanchions, boats and other articles which were carried away by the sea. They "shipped a sea in the main hatch" as well.[23] One can just imagine the chaos as water poured into the ship during the storm. How frightened the passengers must have been. The newspapers stated: "The passengers have, as a matter of course, been greatly alarmed and inconvenienced."[22] They managed to sail to Plymouth, England on 26 November, Captain Pearson deciding it was the best option. Captain Pearson contacted Mr Wilcocks the emigrant agent and then surveyors for Lloyds came on board to survey the damage and do a report.

NEW ZEALAND.—HENRY H. WILLIS and Co.'s LINE of PACKETS.—The following fine, first-class, full-poop vessels will be despatched from the St. Katharine Docks about the undermentioned dates, alternately to the Northern and Southern Settlements of New Zealand :—

Ships.	Tons.	Commanders.	To sail.	Ports.
Cashmere	800	G. Pearson	Oct. 7	Auckland and New Plymouth
Royal Albert	800	A. Scanlan	Oct. 20	Wellington, Nelson, and calling at Otago
Sir E. Paget	800	A. Barclay	In Nov.	Canterbury or Otago and other Ports
Simlah	800	C. Robertson	In Nov.	Auckland and New Plymouth

For freight, passage, or further information apply to Henry H. Willis and Co., insurance brokers, &c., 3, Crosby-square.

The Times (London), 20 September 1852

Archdeacon W. Williams wrote about the journey in a letter. He wrote: "The continuance of contrary winds led us to seek refuge for a time at Falmouth. There being a change for the better, we left that on 21st

November, but within a few hours were met again by a south-west gale just as we had cleared the Lands End. Then we were struck by a heavy sea which carried away our bulwarks and one of our boats, and the damage was so great that we had to put back again. This time we went to Plymouth and the repairs altogether occupied a month. Again we sailed on December 23rd only again to meet with adverse winds, and on 26th December we reached our Harbour again in the midst of one of the most terrific gales which had been experienced since the year 1838. The number of wrecks on every part of the Coast was fearful, and one large Brig went on shore the same evening close to the heads of the harbour, and all hands perished. Our long delay was wearying, but there seemed to be a special providence over us, and without doubt it was wisely ordered that we should be so kept back from our purpose. At last on January 17th, 1853, we were able to get clear off."[24]

It was noted that Plymouth was maybe a better option than London for sending out immigrants. There had been such a terrible time trying to clear the channel that Plymouth would have been a lot easier. It would have also eased the minds of relatives on shore in England and cost less in damage to the ship as well as saving many weeks of wasted time stuck in the Channel.[22]

Many other ships sailed into Plymouth including the Belgian ship *Maria Amelia* and the schooner *Bijon*. The schooner *Anna* of Copenhagen was totally dismasted. A barque was found totally abandoned and was towed by a smack into Fowey and there were many other cases of damage from the bad weather.[23]

It was lucky the *Cashmere* was in port as a hurricane hit on Sunday 25 December causing much destruction. The storm was the worst since 1839, causing much destruction and a "frightful list of casualties" when it came to ships along the coast. The upper portion of the English Channel was the scene of "deplorable events," and at Plymouth where the *Cashmere* had entered the harbour there was a total wreck of a ship called the *Ocean Queen*, of London. The ship was of about 400 tons and due to an error by the Captain it hit one of the dangerous reefs while trying to enter Plymouth Harbour. All the crew perished.[25]

FOR LONDON.

THE FINE A. 1 SHIP "CASHMERE," 640 tons register, George Pearson, commander, having splendid Poop accommodations for Passengers, will sail as above in all March.

Apply to

BROWN & CAMPBELL.

Jan. 29th 1852.

Daily Southern Cross, 23 March 1852 (advertising the return trip after the 1851 journey out to New Zealand)

The *Cashmere* was refitted and this took a long time with the passengers having to wait for their ship to be fixed.[21] Several passengers left the ship due to the storm, leaving more space for others on board. The cuddy in particular had been previously overcrowded.[24]

They finally sailed from Plymouth on 17 January 1853. The journey had fair winds but at the equator were very light breezes and calms which would have slowed their journey down. They sighted Van Diemen's Land (Tasmania) on 24 April 1853[24] and rounded the southern end where heavy gales were encountered. These were blowing ENE to NE.[21]

The ship finally arrived at Auckland on 9 May. The journey took sixteen weeks exactly after leaving Plymouth.[24]

Those in New Zealand were very anxious to know what had happened to the *Cashmere* when it didn't arrive as expected, the journey being 200 days from the first departure from Gravesend to arrival in Auckland. One can only imagine how relatives were suffering, fearing that their loved ones were lost. There were no updates as to the progress of the ship. The facts of the long journey were relayed via the local newspapers to the Auckland locals.[21]

Some passengers were returning to New Zealand after a trip back to their homeland. These people included Venerable Archdeacon William Williams and his family, as well as many friends and family of people already in the Colony.

Archdeacon Williams acted as the ship's chaplain and held church services as well as giving a class in the Maori language for those who wished to learn.[24]

Two deaths and one birth occurred during the voyage. One death was of an adult man named Wright who left a widow and three young children to arrive in a new country with no husband and father. He had started the journey in good health, but tragically became sick and died. The other death was of an infant.[21] The birth wasn't listed in the records.

The ship then travelled on to New Plymouth, Taranaki from Auckland, arriving on 6 July 1853. Passengers from Auckland to New Plymouth were Mr and Mrs Hankin, Mr and Mrs Priske, Mr Towgood, Messrs. Ronald (3).[26]

A Blackwall Frigate similar to the Cashmere *(Northfleet, taken in 1853)*

To Captain PEARSON, ship 'Cashmere.'

Dear Sir,—We cannot take leave of you, without expressing our warmest acknowledgments of the great kindness and attention we have received from you, during our voyage from England in the 'Cashmere.' The circumstance of the rough weather we experienced in the English channel, and the long detention which followed, was trying alike to the passengers and to yourself; but we are glad of this opportunity of bearing our testimony to the unremitting exertions on your part, to alleviate the inconveniences felt, and to promote in every possible way the comfort of all on board. We wish you success in your voyage from this port, and sincerely hope that you will hereafter realize the desire you have expressed of settling in this country.

We remain, dear Sir,
with much esteem,
most sincerely yours,

- Edward Porter,
- Maria Porter,
- Hannah Dilton,
- Henry Hill,
- Isabella Hul,
- George White,
- James Williams,
- William Williams,
- Jane Williams,
- Emma Lanfear,
- Matilda Walker,
- Frances Jones,
- Anna Maria Williams,
- Anne Tomes.

Ladies and Gentlemen,—

Your kind acknowledgments of my efforts to ensure your comfort during the period we have been thrown together, is highly gratifying to me; and I beg to assure you that I shall always retain a grateful sense of your appreciation of my services.

I trust you may all realize your expectations regarding the land of your adoption, and

I remain, your's truly,

G. PEARSON.

Daily Southern Cross 24 June 1853[27]

Captain Pearson Discovers Unknown Islands

On the way back to the United Kingdom from Palmerston North, George Pearson came across some islands that were not on his map about 300 miles east of Cape Melville, Queensland, Australia. He recorded their position and details about them. He saw a beautiful sandy beach and some scrub. He wished to call them Willis's Islands after the owner of his boat Messrs Willis & Co (they actually weren't the owners just the charter company). They can now be found on maps, named as Willis Islets, a series of three islands named North Cay, Mid Islet and South Islet (also called Willis Island). They cover 500 km^2 and are part of a sunken atoll.[28] Willis Island is now the site of a weather monitoring station for the Australian Bureau of Meteorology. It was established in 1921 as a cyclone warning station for Queensland. These days generally three people live on the island and manage the station. They live in a Robinson Crusoe type setting. Absolute paradise![29]

The details of his amazing discovery were published in *The Morning Chronicle* (London) on 17 November 1853 and are written in full below.

"DISCOVERY OF ISLANDS NEAR TORRES STRAIT

"The following account of the discovery of two islands has been sent us by Captain Pearson, of the ship *Cashmere*. On a reference to maps we cannot find any islands laid down near the position assigned, though it is possible that the recent surveys of Captain Stanley may have indicated them, as he was very much occupied about that part of the seas adjacent to Australia. The position assigned by Captain Pearson, namely, lat. 16 deg. 53 min., and long. 149 deg. 51 min E., is about 300 miles east from Cape Melville, and about 200 south of the Louisiade Archipelago, where it is probably that many islands and islets exist which have not yet been laid down in the charts:-

"Report of the *Cashmere*. - The *Cashmere* left New Plymouth, New Zealand on July 12, 1853, on her way to India, via Torres Strait. For the first part of the passage experienced a continuance of heavy squalls and gales of wind from the N.W. with heavy rain until July 28, in lat. 22 deg. 29 min. S., from whence southerly winds, and fine clear weather. On Tuesday, August 2 (civil time), at 8 p.m., saw the Alert reef, and on not being able to weather it, tacked and stood to the southward. At daylight nothing visible from the masthead; bore away to the N.N.W.

"Thursday, August 4, 6 a.m. – Saw two islands covered with bushes, from

18 to 20 feet high, apparently with a fine sandy beach, one bearing N.N.W., the other N.E., by compass, not being marked in any of our charts, nor in Horsburg's Directory. Hauled the courses up, and laid the foreyard to the mast and drifted down mid-channel. At 7 a.m., the following bearings were taken by an azimuth compass: - East Island, north end, N.E. by E. ½ E. East Island, south end, E. by N. ½ N., with heavy breakers extending three or four cables length from the N. W. end. West Island, north end, S.W. by W. ½ W. West Island, South end, S.W. ½ W., also with heavy breakers from the S.W. end. At 8 a.m. bore way N.W. by N. ½ N. Position of the ship at noon by good sights, lat. 16 deg. 22 min. S., long, by chron., 149 deg. 38 min. E., which by course made good since time of bearings places the East Island in lat. 16 deg. 53 min. S., long, 149 deg, 51 min, E., westside West Island, lat 16 deg. 55 min. S., long. 149 deg. 43 min, eastside. Visible from the deck between nine and ten miles. Should the above-described islands not have been previously noticed, I shall call them Willis's Islands, in compliment to the owner of the *Cashmere*.

"Sunday, Aug. 7. – Entered Torres Strait at two p.m., by Raines Island passage, and saw the wreck of a large vessel on the N.E. end of the "Great detached reef," apparently broken in two, mast over the side. An American barque in company, name unknown.

"Wednesday, Aug. 10 – At noon hove to off Booby Island, and sent our report on shore, where saw the vessel wrecked was the *Borneuf*, which struck at two a.m. on the morning of the 3rd, crew taken off by three Dutch vessels, and six by the *Earl Grey,* who reports that the captain of the vessel, his wife, sister and five seamen were drowned. The *Earl Grey* was bound to Bombay, August 7. The American barque still in company, still not able to ascertain her name. After leaving this island had easterly winds and fine weather.

"17th. – Passed between the islands of Timor and Rathe.

"Sept. 4. – Crossed the equator with variable winds and squally weather."

"13th. – arrived of Sandheads and took pilot on board; steamed up the river, and anchored off Calcutta on the 15th."[30]

Willis Island (also known as South Islet), one of the islands discovered by Captain Pearson on the Cashmere in 1853. (Creative Commons Attribution Licence 3.0)

What a career highlight for Captain Pearson this would have been. He was able to name his own islands. One can only imagine the prestige attached to this for a mariner.

1854 Voyage to Auckland and New Plymouth

20 April 1854 – 6 August and 21 August 1854

Captain Pearson must have been on a high after his tropical island discovery but the job went on for him and he had to sail the *Cashmere* back to New Zealand again. The *Cashmere* had a run of 118 days, leaving Gravesend on 20 April 1854. She passed Madeira on 28 April and Crossed the Line on 15 May. On 25 May they were at Lat 26 S and Long 33 W.[31] On 2 June they signalled the ship *Terra Nova* which was travelling from Greenock to Melbourne, out 46 days. From 6 to 10 June the ship did an amazing 1,110 miles! On 9 June, however, there was a tragedy when one of the ship's boys was lost overboard. He fell out of the main rigging as he was coming down.

When the *Cashmere* reached the Cape of Good Hope, she experienced very rough weather. They sighted Van Diemen's Land on 25 July and sighted Mount Egmont on 3 August. The *Cashmere* came into New Plymouth. She was expected to leave New Plymouth on 24 August 1854 for Auckland but she left much sooner than this.[32]

There were 98 passengers on board. Sixty-five got off at New Plymouth and the rest travelled to Auckland arriving on 21 August.

Reverend John Macky wrote a huge diary[33] with much detail about the voyage. The following accounts give a summary of major and interesting events talked about in the diary.[34]

10 and 13 April 1854 and John Macky was leaving for New Zealand. He commented that people were weeping and that they may never see each other again in this life, only in heaven. His wife was depressed and John felt his own "health and peace of mind beginning to suffer."

On 15 April the *Cashmere* was towed from St Katherine's docks to Gravesend by a steamer. There was much confusion on board. The next day passengers went on shore to buy the last supplies needed and Rev Macky was upset to see so many shops open on the Sabbath! He writes: "the Sabbath is very much desecrated here—Steamboats and Railway Trains constantly running, crowds of people on the wharves and in the pleasure gardens in the river steamers all sorts of amusement, fiddlers, harpers etc." On 18 April there was a delay as a new fire engine was put onboard the ship and a Government Inspector was wanting some alterations. They finally left Gravesend on 20 April after Willis and Co. staff came on board to have accounts of freight settled at 4am. On 21 April they saw a British steam cruiser towing a Russian barque that they had captured.

The passengers experienced much sea sickness in the Channel from 22 April to 26 April. Many were weak and miserable. They sailed along the Bay of Biscay, but didn't sight any land. They sighted the island of Madeira on 28 April and noticed how rocky it appeared with a large white building, thought to be a chapel or convent, on the hill. By 29 April everyone was feeling much better.

On 30 April they sighted Palmas Ferros and Teneriffe of the Canary Islands. It was Sunday and Rev Macky preached under an awning on the Quarter Deck. He said that the singing of the passengers was wretched! On 1 May it was very hot and Rev Macky commented on the advantages of a stern cabin as they could have the window open at night and sleep with just a single blanket and sheet. They saw a whale and porpoises but were travelling slowly. They saw a nautilus or Portuguese man-of-war which occasionally raised a tiny sail and glided past them. On 4 May the Rev gave a poetic entry: "Saw two sails today. One crossed our stern, coastward, probably bound for some part of Africa the other ahead of us on the same course as ourselves. How pleasant it is to have the sense of utter loneliness relieved by even the sight of a sail at a distance and how vast must be the ocean on whose bosom so many ships are constantly traversing and yet so seldom falling in with one another."

On either side of the quarter deck were "trusses of hay" for the sheep to eat and when the dew got on it the smell of hay in the evening reminded the Rev of sitting in a beautiful meadow. But then he would come back to reality and his regrets.

On 5 May they passed between the Cape de Verdi islands and a group of porpoises. They next day they saw a whale. On 7 May the Captain treated the cabin passengers to Champagne! A real treat!

On 8 May the first mate Sedgewick harpooned a porpoise and Rev was not impressed at his pride in harpooning animals. Walker, the second mate was described as a nice mild agreeable fellow. The sailors "relished" the dolphin. The passengers also saw many Black Fish which were valuable for their oil.

On 10 May, nearly a barrel of water was collected off the Quarter Deck due to the rain. They saw a vessel from the Blackball Line of Packets which generally sailed to Mauritius. It was sultry and warm and they were at 6.30 North Latitude.

On 11 May a baby was born to Mr and Mrs Shaw. Mr Shaw was in steerage and a servant to Mr Hammerlin. On 12 May they saw and spoke three vessels. On 14 May the Swedish Barque *The Adelaide* was close enough to communicate with the *Cashmere* through the "speaking trumpet." They were travelling from India laden with rice for Cowes. The Captains spoke to each other.

They crossed the line on 12 May at 23 W Longitude. They didn't celebrate the event except for the sailors who were drinking. Rev. Macky was glad the "barbarous practices of former times which I believe are nearly universally exploited" were not practiced on the *Cashmere* this time. On 20 May they were at 13° S Latitude. On 21 May the baby was baptised after the ship, George *Cashmere* Shaw.

On 23 May they passed Trinidad but it was not visible due to it being dark. On 24 May it was so hot that Rev. Macky's boys lay "quite in a state of nudity." On 26 May they spoke with the *Sea Kelpie* from London to Mauritius out 45 days. They also spoke the *Fides* of New York from Callao to London, loaded with guano. Rev. Macky commented that the cards that were being played in the cuddy have "the appearance of evil," and even though there was no gambling going on, he would not go into the cuddy while they were being played. He was finding the voyage extremely dull, but not taking part in the cards wouldn't have been helping!

On 28 May the *Cashmere* was at about 32.30 W longitude but the *Sea Kelpie* reckoned 35 W latitude. One of them was wrong. They sighted some islands. The next day Rev. Macky was in the cuddy when an Irish husband and wife had a huge quarrel which he described as a "sad exhibition" and shook his wife Rebecca's nerves.

Rev. Macky described 30 May as a "dull stupid day." A dolphin was caught by the Boatswain. The next day the ship was travelling faster and there were black birds with stripes on each side visible, apparently called "parsons." Also two Cape Pigeons were seen. They were at Latitude 25.30. On 1 June Rev Macky says, "General harmony prevails but there is a trifling undercurrent of scandal which I do hope will not increase so as to mar our comfort." On 2 June they spoke the *Terra Nova* from Greenwich to Melbourne who had exactly the same longitude as the Captain, which satisfied him. On 3 June the ship was tacking and it was hard to write with the ship so much on one side. This happened for a couple of days and on 6 June there was "pitching" of the ship during the night which made it hard to sleep. They saw albatrosses with wing spans about 6 ft. Some were taken using a hook and line. Suddenly the temperature had changed and everyone needed coats on deck and blankets at night.

It was cold on 8 June and Rev. Macky comments, "I regret to say the Card playing continues and that no good is being done on board in the way of mental, moral or religious improvement by the majority of the passengers."

On 9 June a sailor lad named William James fell and drowned. The third mate named Walker and seven men lowered the lifeboat and tried to save him but their efforts were unsuccessful as there was a heavy sea. William's father had been drowned at sea five months earlier and his mother had asked he not go to sea but he did anyway. Rev. Macky said "and was alas like the majority of sailors a careless thoughtless lad." The passengers were terribly upset and grieving over the loss of William. The Rev. felt a terrible suspense waiting for his rescue and when the call went out that he didn't make it, Rev. Macky wept. The next day he thought about the death and on Sunday he preached about how close to death we all are. That Sunday many did not attend the service as they were trying to catch a flock of birds including pigeons, undertakers, petrels and other birds.

On 13 June Rev. Macky says, "This evening I was rendered very unhappy by hearing unpleasant reports of McL. no one can be trusted. I have never doubted that person." Who this person is has to be deciphered from the passenger list! The only person who might match is Mr. H. MacFarlane.

The next few days were very boring and dull with dull weather, and people's moods seemed dull also. On 20 June there was a gale in the night and the Rev was thankful that his children stayed asleep through it, all except Sam who asked if there was a fear of being wrecked that night. Rev. Macky reassured him and he went back to sleep.

On 27 June there were lots of birds near the ship and a fine albatross which could not be caught with bait. Rev Macky wrote a poem for the drowned sailor.

Drowned

It was a day of wind and rain,
And waves were running high,
And we were sailing on the main
Beneath a Southern Sky.

All hearts were light for hope's bright star
Had shone upon our way,
And pointed to a land afar
Glad with her own bright ray.

Full half our voyage we have passed,
Nor cause for grief we had
And now the full sail beat to the mast,
Who could then well be sad?

Chief of our ship a man of heart,
In duty firm yet bland
Did well perform the Master's part
And well our comfort planned.

His mates were favourites with us all
True British sailors both

The Voyages of the Cashmere

Ever alert at duty's call
To kindness never loth.

The hardy crew with cheerful song
Performed the mild command
Boldly the slippery decks along
Or while aloft they stand.

That day in various past time we
Clothed time in lightest dress
Some gazed upon the troubled sea
Some read Some played chess.

While thus engaged the cry arose
A man is overboard
And still the vessel onward goes
And still the billows roared.

But' 'to' the gallant ship soon 'lies'
Owning the helm-man's power
The revolving lifebuoy swiftly flies
Brave hearts the lifeboat lower.

But all in vain - the struggle's past
The charm of life is o'er.
He looks that awful look, the last
He sinks to rise no more

And who has perished from our sight?
Ah, whose sad fate was this
Whose day has thus dissolved in night?
For misery or bliss.

When first the alarming cry was rained
This was a fearful thought
And wives and mothers Jesus blest
They found the ones they sought.

Ah, he was friendless the lost one,
A lonely sailor boy.
Few tears were shed when he was gone
Little it marred our joy

But the widowed Mother of the lout
Of him oft speaks and prays

Thinking her darling still is tossed
Upon the storm waves.

But when to Merry England's Shore
Our ship again is borne
She learns her son returns no more
Then bitterly she'll morne

And often, often she will tell
Even till she finds her grave
O her son who from the *'Cashmere'* fell
And sank beneath the wave.

But while of the sailor's fate we think
And of his mother's woe
Let us not forget how near the brink
Of the abyss below.

There's but a step 'tween us and death
That hand will seize us all
And mayhap sudden take our breath
Be ready for the call.

On 28 June there was some sort of "scene" between the Captain and Mr Motherell but it was hard to determine what happened from the diary. On 29 June there was a chess match with three people on each side. On one side was the Captain, Mrs. Nixon and Joe Cochrane and on the other was Dr. Sealy, Miss Hinde and the Rev. Macky. On 1 July Rev. Macky reported that his side won using great caution, even though the other side had more talent. Rev. Macky makes a hilarious comment suited to his profession: "By the way in this respect the playing of a game of chess is a very good emblem of what should be the regulation of our conduct at all times. How many ruined men can trace all their misfortunes to one false step taken hastily and without due consideration. Indeed there are very few who have walked so wisely all their lives but as not to have been guilty of some indiscretions which though the evil consequences of them may have been in a great measure retrieved by their after conduct have never the less so far proved injurious as to render them out run and distanced in the race of life by those competitors who acted with greater foresight and produced throughout but more especially at the start."

On 2 July there was a very bad gale and the sea would strike the ship "like the shock a cannon shot would produce." It was a Sunday but Rev. Macky couldn't preach due to the storm. However he did hear that some sailors were reading their Bible's and praying. One wave was particularly bad but they escaped huge damage as only the tail of it struck the ship. The bulwark on one side was broken off. It make a huge sound though, making everyone think there was huge damage. Rev. Macky says: "The *Cashmere* appears to be a good tight ship... she made very little additional water during the storm though it would not be at all surprising if she had. It was to me a matter of surprise that after so much straining she did not leak at every joining and many waves struck her with so much force that I thought them quite sufficient to stave her in." The next day, on 3 July, the storm thankfully abated.

On 4 July the Reverend gave an amazing description of the chaos in the cuddy. "I find I can do very little in the way of reading or writing. Before breakfast there is not time or space. Breakfast is scarcely over when the confusion of preparation for the children's dinner commences and when that is over a very short time intervenes before the Cuddy is again occupied by the Stewards in laying the table for our own dinner and when that is over and dinner past it is almost night and absolutely nothing can be done till after tea and then the noise of the children playing, general conversation and card playing is so great and so incessant that anything requiring much thought is not to be undertaken except to prove a bitter failure. Yesterday some of our children were loud in their complaints that at dinner they had not got a share of some roast pork... but this morning several children were confined with sickness owing to their having eaten plentifully of pork which was under-done... so that the children found it was good for them not to have been permitted to get what they thought it was an injustice to be deprived of. Let me learn patience and contentment from this circumstance."

On 5 July they were 100 miles south of the Island of St Paul and the next day there was another storm during the night and the Reverend alluded to a high up crew member being "in a condition last night disqualifying him for the performance of his duty." Someone was obviously drunk!

On 7 July the ship's carpenter repaired the bulwark so the "*Cashmere* looks herself again." Moses Wallace exchanged for a place in the second cabin where he is much more comfortable and the wind was very favourable.

On 9 July they had snow showers and squalls. Two days later Mrs Carrington, a second cabin passenger gave birth to a stillborn child. A very sad time for her. Rev Macky then wrote a poem for George *Cashmere* Shaw the boy he had baptised on board.

To The Ocean Child

Hail little stranger, child of Ocean
Sleeping on thy mother's breast.
Calmly in the wildest motion
As when winds are sunk to rest.
That morn when first we bade thee welcome
To this moving breathing Earth world
Scarce a cloud was in the welcome
Scarce a breath the waters curled
And lovely was that Sabbath morning
When we met for worship as our wont
In innocence thy meek adorning
They brought you to the sacred font.
And while winds here gently murmuring
Prayer of heaven for thee was made
And for thee unconscious slumbering
Vows were uttered to be paid.
Thy father at thy baptism gave thee
The names our ship and Captain bore
Which with his own may heaven save thee
Make thy name 'George *Cashmere* Shaw'.
The sea on thy natal morn resembled
Thy own placid gentle sleep—
In its fury we have filled with trembling
Deep wildly calling unto deep.

So when you may hereafter often
Be tossed upon life's stormy sea
May God in love the rough winds soften,
When they blow, dear child, on thee

On 13 July Rev. Macky commented that he didn't like the atmosphere of gossip in the Cuddy. "... not a day passes but some new piece of scandal or something approaching it turns up. Sometimes the ladies sometimes the servants... the Captain at one time mixed up in it... Mr. Wetherell at another... Mr. Sedgewick first mate at another. Some all smiles today... will be at daggers drawn tomorrow. Some all compliments and courtesy to an individual when they are defaming on every fitting opportunity."

The next day Rev. Macky was a lot happier, his mood was fluctuating up and down depending on the day and what was going on onboard the ship. He described himself as "distant and morose" while on board.

On 18 July he commented that there was "apprehensions of a storm... Old Mr Hammerton and my father look at the Barometer about every half hour from 7 in the morning till 9 or 10 at night and are sanguine or melancholic according to its rise or fall." Some people were unkindly playing tricks on the old men into thinking a hurricane was coming by fiddling with the barometer. That night there was bad weather with a constant rocking of the ship which kept passengers awake and broke items such as a "potter's vessel." On 20 July Rev. Macky felt the most alarm he had felt since first leaving on the ship. The wind and waves made a "fearful sound" and the ship was travelling at a tremendous pace through the water. There was a shower of hail and then things improved, except the ship started rocking.

On 21 July Rev. Macky attended a sailor who was ill and "anxious of his spiritual state." He was thought to be a dodger, trying to get off work but Rev. Macky thought he was genuinely sick. The next day the weather improved, much to everyone's joy, but this didn't last for long with a high wind coming up the early morning of 24 July. They were expecting to see Van Diemen's Land at 10 am but soon realised they had already passed it. They were at 149° E. About two degrees east of Hobart Town.

On 25 July Rev. Macky wrote: "We thought Mary Jane our servant had been hoaxed by somebody who told her that Van Diemen's Land was in sight... but it turned out to be quite true and that we were in error in supposing we had passed that land yesterday. The truth is the Chronometers were very incorrect and we could not have been less than 8 or 9 degrees astray in reckoning. The consequences might have been awful. Of course supposing we had passed Van Diemen's Land North East as the course we wished to sail and had that night been foggy or wet we would likely have been driven on the land. As it was we had according to the account of the sailors and passengers, a narrow escape although the ship's officers say otherwise. Where the rocks known by the name of 'Eddystone' were seen by the man on watch it is said we were sailing directly towards them and would have been on them in about half an hour. I regard it as merciful providential interposition and I trust we will be truly grateful to our gracious God who did not leave us to be overwhelmed in the waters of the Ocean but has shown us that his arm is mighty to save even when human skill and foresight are utterly at fault."

The next night they saw sheet lightning. Rev Macky commented "Here I sit in my own Cabin writing this Journal and the motion is so great that I can scarcely keep the pen on the paper and my whole body is twisted and wearied excessively with the reeling I am subjected to." He started counting the days before arrival and the journey was a slow as ever!

On 28 July the Reverend wrote another poem.

Farewell

Farewell companions of our Ocean Home
Over 16000 miles of treacherous seas
(Now calm as sleeping child now lashed to foam)
Emblem of life and sinner's destiny.

With breaking hearts and eyes suffused to tears
We bade adieu to England's shore,
Our bosoms torn with various hopes and fears.
Most to behold our native land no more.

By various fates and various fortunes led
To seek another and far distant land,
We dried at length the bitter tears we shed
Trusting our all in the Almighty hand.

And now perforce one family we were
Who must for weeks and months together dwell:
And on each other happiness confer
Or make our ship a very type of Hell.

The weeks and months their rapid course have sped
And though not free from imperfection's strain
Yet yon mild charity, prejudices fled,
And dark distrust and hatred in their train.

And Sabbaths were alliances of love,
Our faith the same... we shared each others forms
And sought together mercy from above
To guide us mid life's dangerous calms and storms

By mutual knowledge, friendships stronger grew,
Until it rivalled even the growth of years:
And kindness, sympathetic bosoms drew,
To tell each other all their hopes and fears.

Thus passed the swiftly flying time away,
Which we had feared would prove distressing long:
And some would gladly have it longer stay
That they might longer be such friends among

'Tis true not alloyed our joys have been

Some trifling bitter mingled with the sweet:
The edge of temper oft is all too keen
And judging too, severer than is meet.

But let this pass... as did those awful gales,
Which for a little filled our hearts with fear
And to life's gentler breezes spread the sails
Hasting to wipe from Sorrow's eye the tear.

Go ever shine where darkness is most dense,
And ever holy principles maintain:
The Tribune God will be your sure defence
And true it is that Godliness is gain.

And now Farewell: Mayhap a long Farewell
May blessings rest upon you from above
And may we all in Heaven Dwell
And sing the praises of redeeming love

But see; your voyage now is almost o'er
And snow capped Egmont rises to our view
Your boats will land you on New Plymouth's shore
And we must say again 'Adieu Adieu'

That day a baby girl was born to Mrs Sealy, the wife of the ship's surgeon. They were both fine. They were going to go on shore at New Plymouth but doubted Mrs Sealy would be well enough so would continue on to Auckland.

The all thought they saw Mt Egmont on 31 July but it was their imaginations and they were still 140 miles away. Rev. Macky commented: "We were amused no little at a walking match between my father and Miss Bell Harriett Hammerton. My father walked best but the air and look of determination and mighty effort exhibited in his countenance and were so like anger that he might be supposed to be resenting an insult or contending with his mortal foe was irresistible and unfilial though it was I laughed immoderately. Mrs. Nixon beat him by a kind of hop step and jump and exalted with triumphant air at her supposed success. She seems in many respects a character.. I hope she will prove on further acquaintance an amiable character... it occurs to me that a long friendship with her will be best secured by a moderate degree of intimacy."

On 1 August Rev. Macky made an interesting comment about the sailors on board: "Had another long conversation with the deaf and dumb boy today and visited the sick sailor in the forecastle where I had an opportunity of talking to and praying with several of the crew. I rather fear the treatment of the sailors in this ship savours too much of a harsh discipline... they are to a man dissatisfied and if they can get it accomplished they will leave this ship at Auckland. I fancy Masters and mates have a good deal to do in making the characters of sailors and that if they did their duty as Christian men the sailors as a class would be of a different stamp."

The next day Mr Carrington, a second cabin passenger, spotted something that looked like land and then John Ferguson, servant to Rev. Macky's father went up to the cradle of the foremast and called out "land land." They finally saw Mt Egmont but very faintly. The next morning on 3 August it was visible "in all its glory." A "magnificent cone with its resplendent snowy mantle shining in the light of the morning sun." That evening was the most magnificent sunset that Rev. Macky thought they would ever see in their lifetime. Mt Egmont was lit up on the apex and it "reflected most resplendently the gilded beams of the glorious sun..."

The next day the mountain was covered with clouds but they saw the forests, fields and houses. They saw three rocks called the Sugar Loaves as they came into the port of New Plymouth. Rev Macky wrote:

"As we neared we could perceive the white houses of New Plymouth which appears a scattered town but very beautifully situated and surrounded by a country which I have no doubt will in a few years merit the appellation given it by Hursthouse... 'The Garden of New Zealand'. Here a pilot comes aboard to point out the best anchorage and we shortly saw a boat leaving the shore but while expecting to see it near us heavy squalls to the westward were gathering and some of the men who were aloft reefing the mizzen saw the boat turn again towards the shore. Indeed our Captain had little expectation of being able to anchor as the glass was falling and the wind blowing on the shore. It was tantalizing and the New Plymouth passengers were very much cast down about it as they fully expected to be on shore in an hour or so. The circumstance of having no harbour will ever be a serious drawback to the prospects of New Plymouth and I believe if parties were aware of this to its full extent they would be discouraged from immigrating to it at all. However for rural life it is probably unsurpassed and those who are willing to give up other things for rural beauty, retirement and quietude will doubtless find here, if anywhere, those wished for blessings realized. The evening wore rather a stormy aspect and with close reefed topsails and sailing close to the wind we are heading at 9 o'clock P.M. North West by West. Another Brig wishes to get anchorage at New Plymouth from where we can't tell is also standing off from land."

On 5 and 6 August they tacked a lot to avoid going back out to sea and were finally anchored at about 10 am on 6 August. Mr Nash, the agent for Willis and Co. came alongside and then had breakfast with the cabin passengers. He had only been in the colony for about six weeks himself, arriving on the *Eclipse*.

On 7 August the boat made three trips to the beach and back to the *Cashmere* taking out goods and passengers. Mrs Sealy went onshore in her cot and Dr Sealy had gone on shore the previous day and found them some accommodation. Some people left without saying goodbye. Maybe they were anxious to get to their new land and forgot their manners.

On 8 August Rev. Macky went on shore and did not think the Maori people that he saw were strange as he had read about them and they seemed familiar to him. "A few days previous a dispute had arisen between two of the tribes on an agrarian question and 16 persons of the tribe friendly to the Europeans were shot... seven of whom have since died. These people were working at a road through the bush for the settlers when the hostile tribe whose Chief is a fractious mob orator sort of a fellow ordered them to desist which they would not do and after first firing over them and then in the ground they fired among them when the result was as stated above. The old friendly Chief and his son were both mortally wounded. The Chief died in hospital and was buried yesterday in the burying place of his fathers. I believe the funeral was rather an imposing spectacle. There were but few of the natives in town today and I learned that the reason was that the road was Tapu or made sacred on account of the outrage. They are boiling with indignation and the hostile Chief is expected to be soon the victim of their revenge. He is said to be very low in spirits and some are of the opinion that he will commit suicide."

On 9 August the *Cashmere* went to sea again with Mr Sedgewick, in command arriving at Auckland on 21 August 1854 with 33 passengers.

1855 Voyage to Lyttelton and New Plymouth

2 July 1855 – 23 October and 22 November 1855

The *Cashmere* was once again commanded by Captain Pearson to New Zealand. The journey had what was considered a fair passage of 101 days and had 160 assisted immigrants on board including about 60 children. There was no description of the voyage in the newspapers, being probably quite uneventful. There are no known diaries for this voyage.

H. H. WILLIS & CO.'s
LINE OF PACKETS
BETWEEN
LONDON AND NEW ZEALAND.

THE following fine first-class Ships are intended to be continued as Regular Traders:—

'Cresswell,' W. O. Barnett, ... 700 Tons.
'Cashmere,' G. Pearson, ... 850 "
'Maori,' C. G. Petherbridge,........ 900 "
'Dolphin,' Turnbull,................. 500 "
'Stately,' T. Ginder,................ 700 "
'Josephine-Willis,' Canney, ...1000 "
'Simlah,' Allan, ... 700 "
'Joseph Fletcher,' Foster,.......... 800 "
'Thetis,' Pook, ... 700 "

The Undersigned, Agents for the above splendid line of Vessels, are authorised to arrange with settlers here who may be desirous of bringing their friends in Great Britain out to this Colony, and are prepared either to pay the Passage Money at once to them, or to give satisfactory security for its payment on arrival of the Vessel.

Further particulars on application to
BROWN & CAMPBELL.

Daily Southern Cross 23 October 1855

The ship carried news to New Zealand of the Crimean War, particularly an attack by allied troops on the Malakhoff Tower and news that the Redan had been repulsed by the Russians. There had been 1473 English troops killed or wounded.[35]

The passengers on this voyage were described by Captain John Parsons of the Lyttelton Harbour Office. He said, "they appear a decent lot" and the Captain of the *Cashmere* spoke of them "very well."[36] They included Mr Watson and family of Hull, the Ray family, G. Hepworth, J. Austin, W. and A. Cameron and A. Rose according to correspondence sent from England.[37]

Mr Franks was schoolmaster on the vessel with another schoolmaster Mr Harkins being sent out to the colony and a schoolmistress Mrs Harkins.

> To the Passengers per Ship
> "CASHMERE."
> THE Undersigned believing that a Person on board the Ship *Colchester*, on her Passage from Melbourne to Port Victoria, had a Parcel containing a Portrait for him, requests that it may be forwarded by Post, first opportunity.
> JAMES WILKINSON, Cabinet Maker, &c.,
> Willis street, Wellington.

Lyttelton Times, 21 November 1855

Mr Harman in London sent a letter to the Superintendent stating that Mr Godley had received a letter from New Zealand stating that a credit had been opened in Godley's name with the Union Bank of Australia for the purposes of emigration to the colony. This was going to allow them to "carry on operations with some degree of certainty."[38]

The ship left for New Plymouth on 15 November 1855 with the passengers being Mr. Atkinson, Miss Crompton, Miss Skinner, Mr. and Mrs. McNaughten and Mr. Hunt,[39] They arrived on 22 November at New Plymouth. The ship then swiftly left on 24 November for China.[40]

Captain George Pearson was named as "our old friend" in the Daily Southern Cross newspaper and so greatly was he admired that they stated "We trust, therefore, that "our old friend" is by this time nearly half way on his voyage to China."[41]

New Colonists

For a great example of what some new colonists went through, the following families are very interesting. William Ivory arrived in 1855 with William Stapleforth, his brother-in-law, and they backpacked their belongings over the Bridle Path to Ferrymead. Ivory's first swag consisted of a seventy pound feather bed, which he carried up the hill one morning before breakfast! The two men inspected maps at the land office and decided to go out to Rangiora and when they arrived, there was just flax, toitoi and tussock with a few pit-sawyers working in the bush. They bought a small-holding each from Torlesse, and Ivory bought a rural section as well.

Ivory found timber and built a simple three-room lean-to, a popular type of cottage which could be added to later. There was a living room in the centre and a fire place big enough to contain a camp oven. The Ivory family moved in to the cottage but soon after were shaken up by an earthquake which made them flee outside in fear and spend the night under the stars. A while later, after the earthquake, was a NW gale of huge ferocity, which imprisoned the family indoors. William Ivory made the decision to go out just once during the wind, crawling on hands and knees to a nearby V-hut where two newly arrived young Englishmen were sheltering in fear for their lives. William gave the young men some food. The Ivory family found that their camp oven, which was kept outside, had been blown several chains away, such was the force of the gale!

William Ivory planted vegetable seeds which he had brought with him on the ship and when the first radishes were ready to eat they had a thanks giving with the family dressed in their best clothes. Ivory said, "After grace which I said with fervour I had not before nor have I since equalled, my heart being so full of gratitude to The Giver Of All Good, we sat on our Canterbury blocks (blocks cut from trees in the bush) around our rough-made table and enjoyed those few simple radishes as though they were a royal feast."[42]

1857 Voyage to New Plymouth and Auckland

19 Dec 1856 - 5 April and 14 April 1857

The *Cashmere* arrived at New Plymouth on 5 April 1857. The majority of the passengers were for Auckland but 25 landed at New Plymouth. The ship sailed the same day for Auckland. The journey was uneventful having a fair passage of 109 days. They had light and fine weather through the voyage. They crossed the Equator on 20 January and the meridian of the Cape on 23 February. The run was good until Van Diemen's Land but then they had baffling winds between there and the New Zealand coast which slowed them right down.[43]

The journey between New Plymouth and Auckland was "somewhat tedious" with severe weather encountered off the North Cape.[43]

In 1857 the *Cashmere* again arrived with European and Colonial news but had left seven days after the mail steamer, so the news was of little importance. There were several old colonists on board the ship. One was T. S. Forsaith Esq., who had travelled back to England to lecture about Auckland to the British public. Obviously Auckland had got a bad name. Whether this was due to the Maori Wars or some other reason, it is not mentioned. Forsaith had apparently helped generate a healthy stream of immigration into the Province. Mr McElwain also returned to the colony on the *Cashmere*.[44]

1859 Voyage to Lyttelton

11 June 1859 – 11 October 1859

The Voyage of the *Cashmere* in 1859 took 121 days. They spoke no vessels and had moderate weather, with the only problem being a lack of good wind to speed their passage. They reached the Snares (some rocky islands just south of Stewart Island) on 4 October and Banks Peninsula on Friday 7 October.

There were quite a few passengers onboard, numbering about 207 but 16 died on the voyage. There were three births during the voyage, which made the final number arriving in Lyttelton about 184 passengers.

Mr. C. W. Fooks, Captain Fuller, Mr W. G. Fuller (of Otago) and other returning settlers were on the ship. Fitzgerald, emigration agent in London stated: "There are onboard this ship a (list?) of as fine names as can be obtained - some with discharges from the army works corps in the Crimea - all from the Westminster Bridge works."[45]

The high number of deaths on board was investigated by the authorities but there were no infectious diseases that caused the deaths. There were two suspicious deaths however. A man named Belaminar, a native of Austria died "under peculiar circumstances" although these circumstances were not outlined in the records. Also a young boy George Davidson died, his death possibly by "severe castigation received at the hands of his father."[46]

List of Births and Deaths

Births
14 Jul   the wife of Josiah King of a daughter
14 Sep   the wife of James Frazer of a daughter
3 Oct   the wife of Donald Munro of a son
Deaths
26 June   John de la Mare aged 2 years

1 July	Emma Gray aged 3 years
2 July	John Cox aged 7 months
6 July	Bruce Craighead aged 7 weeks
7 July	Margaret King aged 1 year 9 months
19 July	George Davidson aged 6 years
21 July	Jane, wife of Josiah King, 26 yrs. of puerperal fever
24 July	Jane Lack King, infant daughter of the above aged 10 days
27 July	Robert Atkinson aged 6 years
28 July	James Graves aged 1 year 8 months
30 July	Charles Atkinson aged 11 months
7 August	Frances Sinclair aged 22 years of consumption
16 September	Albert de la Mare aged 10 months
27 September	Isabella, wife of Robert Atkinson, aged 38 years of diarrhoea.
29 September	Frank Bellminar, aged 29 years.
1 October	Elizabeth Anderson, aged 10 months.

George Davidson's Death

George Davidson was a whiney six year old child. He was unwell during the voyage with diarrhoea and had this problem for the three weeks leading up to his death.

The serious charge of "undue chastisement" causing death was put against the father. The surgeon Henry Horsford Prins gave evidence.

On 19 July Dr Prins was called by George's father to attend to George who was lying on the main hatch gratings and was very ill. When Dr Prins arrived, George had already died. The Doctor had spoken to George's father a week before George's death about chastising the child when he was in such a weak state. The father told Dr Prins he had not "flogged" the child since being warned.

It was determined by post mortem that George had died by rupture of the spleen caused, in his opinion, by injuries to his body. The father was called in to see the internal and external marks of violence on his son. The Doctor asked the father the next day to show him the instrument with which he punished his son, which turned out to be a leather strap.

The injury could have caused death three of four days after it was received as there seemed to be blood let out internally for some time before the day he died.

Edwin Hope was brought to give evidence, his berth being about twelve yards from George's family. He heard blows about three days before the death with what sounded like a rope. After going to see what was going on he saw George lying on the floor dying. He had been told that the child cried at the least thing. Edwin had never seen anyone ill-treat George.

The father gave a statement that his child had got sick on the voyage and was constantly crying for proper food which of course could not be obtained on the ship. He wasted away over a period of three weeks. On the day George died he was brought up on deck because of the stagnant air below. According to the father, George had fallen with his back against a spar alongside the hatch and was breathing heavily.

Several passengers including Louisa Mary Sparey and several others stated they had never seen him ill-treat George.

William Sparey saw George fall down the hatchway stairs the day before he died but the boy would not tell his father. He got up and sat on the hatchway and cried. His father got him some food but George just would not eat and died the next day. He had seen George get beaten with a strap but not severely.

Robert Barrett also confirmed the fall and was present at the post mortem examination and saw a black mark on each side of the body as if from a fall. He said the accused father always behaved kindly to his children.

The case was dismissed, with George's death being put down to his fall down the hatchway, but one has to wonder if the beating had added to the speed of his death. The Surgeon certainly considered the boy had internal injuries from several days earlier.[47]

Testimonial

A testimonial for Captain Byron was written by the first and second class cabin passengers as follows:

"*The Cashmere.*

We have much pleasure in giving publicity to the following address, which was presented by the passengers per Cashmere to the captain, a few days before landing:-

"*Ship Cashmere, October 6, 1859.*

"*To Captain Byron.*

"We, the undersigned first and second class passenger of the Cashmere, beg to offer you our sincere thanks for the care and attention you have bestowed on us, and to express the confidence felt by us in the ability and unceasing vigilance shown by you as commander of the vessel during our voyage from London to Port Lyttelton.

"We would also convey our grateful acknowledgements to Mr. Appleton, the chief mate, and the other officers, for the courtesy we have uniformly received at their hands.

"We are, sir, your obliged and obedient servants."

[Signed by Messrs. Filleul, Fooks, Fuller, Millton, and 30 other passengers.

"Captain Byron has returned the following reply:-

"Ship Cashmere, Oct. 8.

"To the Cuddy and 2nd Class Passengers, on board the Cashmere.

"I have much pleasure in acknowledging your kind testimonial handed me this day: and as your comfort and happiness appear to have been promoted by my endeavours, permit me to say that, after all, with a desire to make your voyage agreeable, and I assure you I feel compensated by your good opinion for any labours which I have undergone. The confidence you have entertained in me, together with your agreeable companionship will be retained in my remembrance, while life and memory hold together. I would also add that through your correspondence either directly or indirectly with Messrs. Willis, Gann. And Co., they will be equally pleased to know that such a good understanding and tranquillity prevailed on board the Cashmere, not withstanding the unavoidable losses sustained among us. I could hope our voyage had been shorter; but as with the assistance of our Divine Protector I have brought you to your adopted land in safety, may you individually continue in good health; may you succeed in every desire you entertain speedily; and if at times you have been rudely or roughly used by the rolling of the ship, still I hope you will never have cause to regret that the Cashmere brought you to the colony of New Zealand.

"I remain, Ladies and Gentlemen,

"Your obedient servant,

"JOHN BYRON."[48]

Enquiry into the condition of the *Cashmere*

There was an enquiry held once the *Cashmere* was in New Zealand as to the condition of the ship with officials D. Donald, Latter and P. Luck present. Evidence was given by Dr Henry Horsford Prins and Captain Byron of the *Cashmere*.[49] This was possibly also part of a court case between Captain Byron and Dr Prins, with Captain Byron accusing Prins of neglect and incompetency.

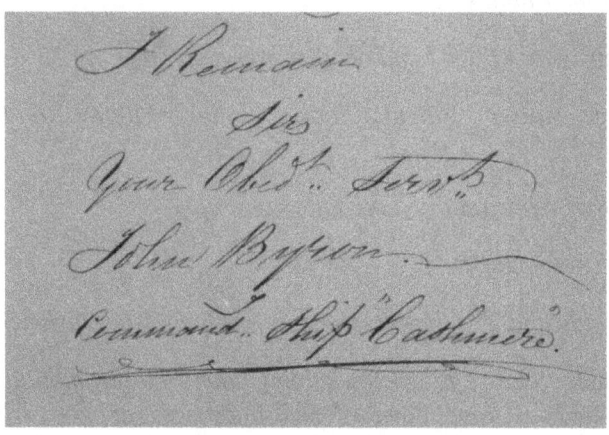

The newspapers suggested a death on board could have been avoided if Dr Prins had done his job, and neglect was suggested. It could have been the death of George Davidson or maybe sailor Frank Bellminar (Belaminar) but names were not mentioned. The Captain had no time for Dr Prins after this event which was only alluded to in the newspapers.

Dr Prins was present at the muster of the passengers on board the ship which took place before an Emigration officer and Medical Inspector. Before the inspection even began Dr Prins had objected to two families boarding. One had whooping cough and the other had measles. Dr Prins told the Medical Officer and Mr Gann (of the charter company) and the families were sent on shore. Subsequently the father and son of the family with measles returned on board and the father, son and daughter of the whooping cough family as well. They left quite a few family members behind on shore who came on the different ship at a later date. The ones allowed back on board were quite well, but after a week on board one of the children was taken ill with whooping cough and the other two days later with measles.

Dr Prins examined the medicine chest and found the quantities to be correct but the amount of medical comforts to be quite short, the illness on board not helping this. He had a slip of paper from the Captain with quantities of medical comforts which included Arrow Root, Sago, Brandy, Wine and Porter. Alcohol was considered a necessary medicine for the sick in those days!

Dr Prins had not received a copy of the Passenger Act until six weeks into the voyage. At the beginning of the voyage he only received notice of his remuneration which was 35 pounds, 15 pounds in advance and the balance on arrival if he did his duties well. After reading the rules he noticed there were no safety lamps on board. The Captain said they had none and would not make them. Eventually the Captain gave "his original lamp in consequence of a disagreement." The passengers had been complaining to the Doctor that the lighting of the ship was poor.

Dr Prins tried to use his medical comforts sparingly. He went through six dozen pints of stout before they crossed the line. The Captain did allow a further supply in two instances. The wine and spirits lasted quite well and also the arrow root and sago. The soup however ran out, there being only 6 dozen half pint tins of soup available for the ill passengers. The Captain refused to provide more and the Doctor had to obtain remnants of soup from the cuddy table (where it appears the second class passengers dined). The Doctor, not knowing what to do, now recommended that mothers of sick children go to the Captain and beg for more supplies. The Captain was offended by this as he could not remedy the situation. However, the Captain himself stated in the evidence that he never refused soup and it was obtained from the 2nd class passenger stores and the steward frequently gave the Doctor soup.

One other issue on the ship was that Mr Greaves, a steerage passenger, had bad conduct on board, but generally the female emigrants were well behaved and there was no immorality. Their compartment was placed beyond the married persons' compartment and they had to pass through to get there. The ship was clean and well ordered, although the cleanliness of the single men's cabins was not great. The Doctor was told about the six o'clock inspection.

The Captain had complained to the Doctor about the schoolmaster neglecting his duties and he was told if he didn't perform satisfactorily the Captain would withhold his certificate. The Captain made sure the Doctor was keeping a close eye on the schoolmaster (William Pearce) and Matron (Mary Fletcher) to make sure their jobs were done sufficiently well.

The Doctor kept a diary of patients and their illnesses but it was destroyed at the Cape in some sort of accident.

The key for the ship's chest went missing at one point. On 3 August 1859 the Doctor had used up all the 7 units of opium, which he used to make tinctures with brandy. The Captain refused, more as his previous surgeons had treated patients without opium. He did not wish to give any out. The Doctor wanted to pull into a port somewhere to get some but the Captain refused. On 22 September, however, the keys to the ship's chest were given to the Doctor and he was allowed the medicines again. He was not allowed any gin for the passengers however, only brandy and wine. It appears that the Doctor and Captain had a bit of friction during the voyage![49]

The court case between the Doctor and Captain was summarised in the newspapers in two separate articles and reiterated the friction between the two men:

"PRINS V. BYRON. This was a demand for £20, balance of wages due to plaintiff, as surgeon of the *Cashmere*; also a claim was entered for legal discharge from the ship, for certain compensation allowed under the Merchant Seaman's Act, and for incidental costs and expenses. Plaintiff produced the agreement with Willis, Gann & Co., under which he came out as surgeon in the *Cashmere*. Plaintiff also produced a letter from defendant. He had signed articles as surgeon. The captain told him his discharge was not necessary, and that he would not pay the balance of wages until a case pending in Court had been settled. Defendant said he was captain of the *Cashmere*; he did not consider plaintiff had properly performed the duties of surgeon, he did not enforce cleanliness between decks. The schoolmaster about four weeks after sailing drew his attention to the want of cleanliness among the single men. Plaintiff saw to this himself. Gave plaintiff printed copies of orders in council. Plaintiff never had bedding taken up to be aired. Did not enforce the order to muster on Sunday. Lent plaintiff instructions to surgeons; Passengers' Act, drawing his attention to sec. 60, Ship's officials Log produced; letters and extracts read, complaining of regulations not being carried out. Defendant here made a long statement as to removal of two sailors from the men's hospital, and placing a female there. Several entries in the log were read relating to use of hospital and cleaning between decks. Plaintiff was always supplied with medical comforts for sailors on application to defendant. Defendant said he believed if there had been greater attention to cleanliness there would have been less illness on board. George Kirkhouse, second cabin passenger, said he had seen plaintiff, below, but did not know, whether in execution of his duty never gave witness any orders. Had heard the captain speak about taking bedding on deck, not the plaintiff; so far as medical attendance was concerned believed plaintiff did his duty. The cabin had been uncleaned on two or three wet days. Robert Atkinson, steerage passenger, said—my wife was ill on board and lay in her own berth. Plaintiff attended her. The only fault I found was her non-removal to the hospital. The between decks' were cleaned every day. Plaintiff never spoke to me about cleaning my berth. Plaintiff gave orders for an extra clean up as we were about coming to an anchor. Further hearing adjourned till 12 o'clock on Friday, yesterday."[50]

"RESIDENT MAGISTRATE'S COURT.

Lyttelton—Friday, Oct. 28.

(Before John Hall, Esquire, R.M.) PRINS V. BYRON.

This case, which was adjourned from Monday last, and the earlier portion of which has been already reported, was an action brought by the surgeon of the ship *Cashmere* to recover salary for his services during the voyage, and to obtain a legal discharge, he having signed the ship's articles. The defence set up consisted of charges of neglect and incompetency alleged against the plaintiff by the defendant, who is master of the *Cashmere*. The Plaintiff's explanatory statement respecting the counter charges was heard this day. He stated on oath that the entries in the official log were not read over to him at the time they purported to have been so read that Captain Byron had never accused him of neglect till after the death occurred of the person alluded to; and that he had always carefully attended to the cleanliness of ship and passengers. He denied having had a copy of the 'Orders in Council,' at the beginning of the voyage. Several passengers by the *Cashmere* from the second cabin and steerage compartments being called upon, gave evidence generally corroborating the plaintiff's statement, especially as to his care in visiting the various compartments, and giving directions about cleanliness, and attending, upon the sick. Some passengers had observed a coolness grow up between the doctor and captain towards the close of the voyage. Dr. Donald, Provincial Surgeon and Immigration Officer, stated that he had visited the *Cashmere* on her arrival, and in consequence of finding that several deaths had occurred on board, had held an investigation on the ship. Complaints were made against the plaintiff similar to those which were now preferred, but on enquiry they seemed to be unsubstantiated. The passengers spoke highly of the plaintiff's attention of as medical officer. The ship was free from unpleasant smell, and though not quite clean, seemed to be a difficult ship to keep so. As to the charge of removing persons from the hospital, witness was of opinion that there might exist good medical reasons for such a step in certain cases. Mr. Hall ordered the discharge applied for to be given, and gave judgment for plaintiff for £20, and costs."

Lyttelton Barracks

It appears many of the *Cashmere* passengers had to stay in the barracks for a long time. There was no quarantine ground as yet in Canterbury. A letter was written on 4 November 1859 by Donald regarding the long stay:[51]

Sir

From the unusual amount of illness in the Cashmere and the length of time it has been necessary to keep some of the immigrants in barracks at Lyttelton it is absolutely necessary to have the rooms lime washed before next vessel arrives.

I have the honour to be your obedient servant.

Wm. Donald, Immigration Officer.

Telegraph Cargo

The *Cashmere* shipped some cargo which was for a telegraph that was being erected between Lyttelton and Christchurch, so a very important cargo indeed. Other parts had been shipped on the *Mary Anne*.[52]

Luggage of a typical immigrant

William Roles was a man who decided to emigrate to New Zealand but at the last minute couldn't board through no fault of his own. His luggage was mistakenly transported all the way to New Zealand on the *Cashmere* and was to be held until he sailed on the next ship.[53] However William later decided not to come at all, his luggage having to be sent back to England.[54] His luggage is a great example of the size of luggage sent out on immigrant ships.

He owned a chest made of elm, non-painted, of the dimensions of 3 ft. 6 in long, 2 ft. deep, 2 ft. broad. As well as a canvas bag, sewn up and corded.

Departure

The *Cashmere* stayed in port for a long time, being loaded with wool from the latest season. In mid December the ship received her first bale of wool on board. This was the first of the season's produce yet shipped. They ran it up to the yard-arm, then the ship hoisted her colours and fired a gun.[55] On 16 December 1859 the *Cashmere* was dressed in colours and fired its guns in a salute for the 10th anniversary of the formation of the settlement.[56]

The *Cashmere* departed Lyttelton on 13 March 1860 for London with Captain Byron at the helm. There were several passengers including cabin passengers Mrs Laurie and five children and steerage passengers, Mr, Mrs and Miss Gosling, Mrs Spencer and two children, Mr Baron, Mr Wilkinson, Mr Taylor, Mr. FitzGerald and Mr. Riggs.[57]

New Advertisements.

FOR LONDON.

THE British Built Ship CASHMERE, A 1, 574 tons Register, John Byron, Commander, daily expected, will be ready to receive cargo early in November.

This ship has superior accommodation for both first and second cabin passengers.

For particulars of freight or passage, apply to
DALGETY, BUCKLEY. & CO.

Lyttelton Times, 10 September 1859.

FOR SALE,

SHIP 'CASHMERE'S STEERAGE FITTINGS. Apply to
DALGETY, BUCKLEY & CO.

Lyttelton Times, 19 October 1859.

Map of the Journey of the *Cashmere*

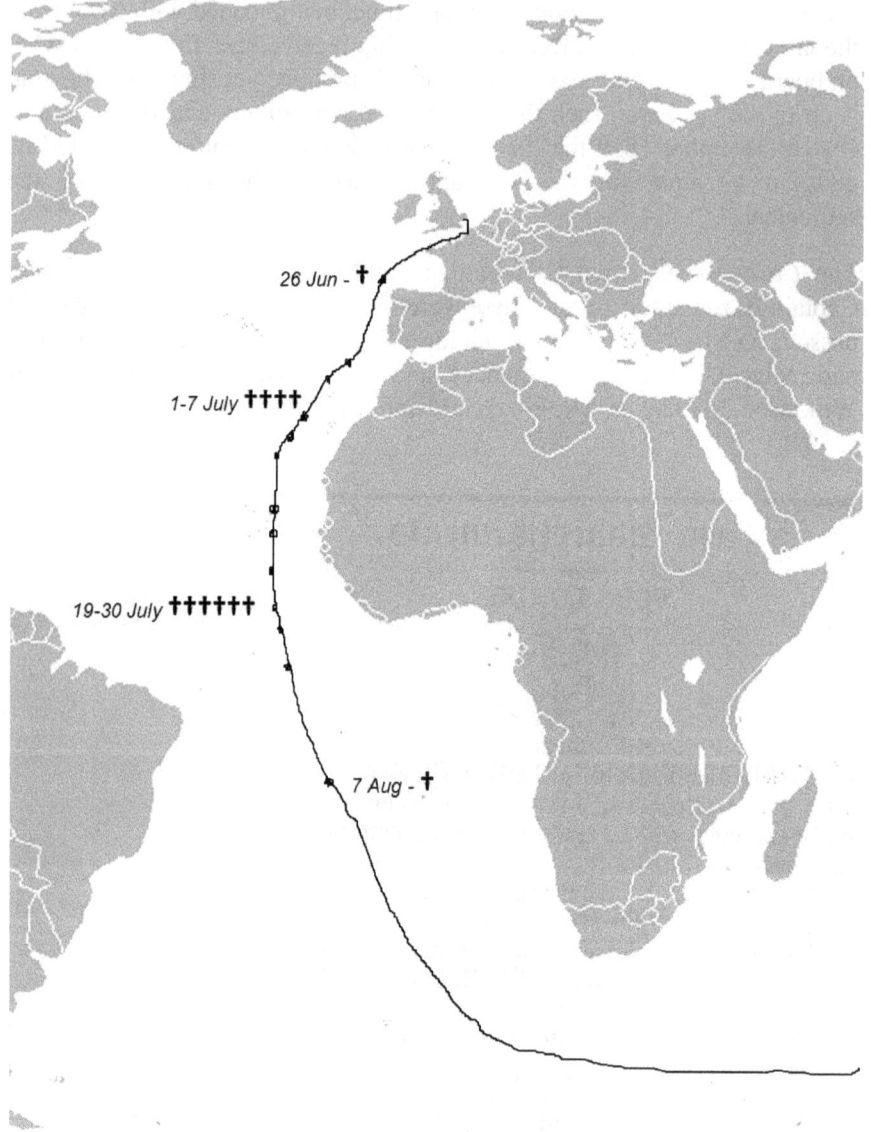

(11 June 1859 – 11 October 1859)

1861 Voyage to Port Chalmers and Lyttelton
1 November 1860 – 9 February and 15 February 1861

The *Cashmere* travelled to Port Chalmers and then Lyttelton in 1861 with Captain Petherbridge in command. It took 102 days to travel to Otago. She was now under the charter of Messrs. Shaw, Savill and Co. and no longer Willis, Gann and Co.

There were only a few passengers on board as well as seven horses shipped from London, - four died on the voyage out, including one horse for Mr. G. H. Moore of Glenmark. She had a full cargo.[58]

One of the passengers was a Mr. James Jones, son of Mr. John Jones of Otago. James had been in England for quite a long time and was returning home on the *Cashmere*. He was the one who had six horses on board including four entires and two mares. A "splendid mare" which was nearly a thoroughbred and a fine chestnut horse of the hunting breed both died of inflammatory colds during the early part of the voyage,[59] in the Bay of Biscay.[60] One can imagine the sorrow as they threw the bodies overboard.

Engraving of French racehorse Chamant from Illustrated London News, May 1877. After painting by John Sturgess (d. 1903)

The other mare that had the same complaint survived until only about a week or ten days before the end of the voyage. The weather upset her and she died and was thrown overboard on 30 January. It was a great loss to the owner and the colony. Three stallions remained and were described as "noble horses." It appeared that Mr Jones had suffered similar losses in the past while trying to bring out horses to the colony.[59]

The ship sailed on for Lyttelton and arrived on 15 February 1861.[61]

1862 Voyage to Auckland

15 December 1861 – 7 April 1862

The 1862 voyage of the *Cashmere* to Auckland was extremely interesting as it left with many English birds for importation into New Zealand. The varieties on board included blackbirds, linnets, thrushes, skylarks, several varieties of duck, mallard and varieties of geese. Sadly one third of the birds died during the voyage.[62] Captain Petherbridge was to transport many more birds to New Zealand on the *Napier* in 1863 and the *Countess of Kintore* in 1870.

John James Wilson was in charge of the birds on the *Cashmere*. He wrote a journal of the voyage. Some of the highlights of the journey are summarized below.[63]

The *Cashmere* was towed from the inner docks in London to the outer gates at 7am on 8 December 1861. They started for Gravesend the next day at 5pm and arrived at 9.30pm. There were some contrary winds and after many attempts the ship finally set sail from near the Hove on 15 December 1861. They passed through Dover Straits at 1.30pm with the ship rolling and pitching about fearfully. Anything not tied down was rolling about, including pots and pans. Nearly everyone was seasick but John was ok.

On 17 December they sighted the Isle of Wight and the pilot left them on 19 December. That day there was a heavy sea. They saw Start Point the next day and everyone waved goodbye to England. The ship was rolling very much that day and some of the passengers were struggling to cope.

On Sunday 22 December it was a nice day and John cleaned out all the birds. The rough weather meant they had been not attended to as much for two or three days. The next day there was no wind all day and a dance was held in the evening.

On 24 December there was a "quite a row on board" because the Captain would not allow supplies of fresh meat for Christmas day. The only thing extra was ¼ lb. of plums and a little more flour for each person. To make plum pudding!

On Christmas Day John made an interesting entry:

"Christmas Day & a more wretched one I never spent. Everyone on board was savage & dissatisfied & well they might be. Fancy salt junk or horse as its called & a hard pudding with about 2 dozen plums in it for a Xmas dinner. I was better off as Fanny was kind enough to make me a duff. I retired to my bunk & did a rare feed all to myself."

It rained a lot that day and the sea was very rough and the boat heaving with gale force winds. While trying to sleep John could hear the wind whistling and the waves thumping the side of the ship. It took a long time but eventually he got to sleep. It was not a great Christmas Day!

On 27 December they signalled a ship bound for St Domingo from France.

On 28 December and it was hot and nearly everyone was asleep on deck or reading.

On the 1st day of 1862 several large whales came close to the ship and one man managed to hit one on the back with a beer bottle, it was so close. The next day it was hot and the ship becalmed. John took his shoes and stockings off as it was much too hot. He wore nothing but a straw cap, shirt and trousers and even that was too much for him. On 3 January they saw a large shoal of porpoises.

On 5 January they spoke the ship Epsom from London to the Cape of Good Hope.

It was very hot weather until 7 January when the sea became heavy and the wind strong. John's beloved straw hat was blown into the sea as he got a huge ducking by the waves. The foretopsail came away during the night due to the strong wind. They were 15 degrees from the line on 8 January.

On 10 January several people lay on deck to try and sleep. At 4am they were awoken when a sailor yelled "Sail on port bow" and after straining his eyes, John could see a large ship in the distance. On 12 January they saw three sharks very close to the ship.

On 17 January they sighted six ships and signalled one going back to London. The next day they saw many flying fish and a dolphin was caught and cooked for dinner. John tried some "for the novelty of the thing" and liked it! They celebrated crossing the line on 19 January.

John gave an interesting account of the fighting and meals on board on 20 January.

"Today's proceedings commenced with a regular row amongst the Irish. When roused they fight like devils & hit anybody who comes in their way no matter whether friend or foe so long as they get a smack at somebody.

Fights & quarrels are by no means an uncommon thing, there's not a meal without a row. It all begins by "Chaffing" one another. We are divided int7 messes, one of each mess acts as Captain for one week & then each takes his turn. The Captain of a mess draws all stores from the steward & sees to the cooking of them etc. I belonged to the 2nd division No 6 mess. We were originally 10 in a mess but we found out that some 2 or 3 of the chaps used to make cakes etc. on the quiet out of the mess stores & so the rest of us kicked up a row & divided the mess into 2 divisions & an awful mess it was as far as regards the cooking. Fellows used to try experiments with salt junk to see if it could be made any more palatable & I need not add that very few were successful."

John mentioned that the heat was making the pitch boil in the cracks on the deck and the tar run down the rigging and masts. John enjoyed watching men run like "a cat upon hot bricks" while trying to walk in bare feet on the sunny deck. On 22 January several men were singing as they couldn't sleep and the sailors stopped them, doused them with seawater and hauled them around the deck by a rope tied to the leg. They also blacked their faces. This went on until near daylight.

The amusements on board were listed as dancing, singing, card playing, dominoes, quoits (made of rope), tossing for money or tobacco, wrestling, climbing ropes, chaffing, boxing and sometimes a fight.

On 27 January some bugs were found in the single women's berth and there was much commotion. There was a scrubbing and bug hunt two days later and many were found.

On 28 January they signalled the *Lurline* bound from Liverpool to Buenos Ayres.

On 1 February a large dolphin was caught. On 2 February passengers and even crew were suffering from the heat. Some women had fits, prickly heat rash and the children ill. On 5 February poor John had his foot lanced by the Doctor. He had poisoned it while running around the deck bare foot! The next day it was getting colder and extra blankets were brought out. On 8 February they were at 40° S, 12° E.

On 13 February the Captain decided to go much further south to catch the better winds. They caught a large porpoise which measured 6 feet 6 inches long and weighed 3 cwt. It was not wasted but cooked the next day

On the night of 14 February it was very rough and this lasted all of the 15th but improved on 16th. On 17 February they were at 46° S, 10° E. On 18

February the ship was sailing on its side but this was better than it rolling. On 20 February, however, John was in his berth being sent to the head and then to the bottom of his berth. He was sleepy but there was no way he could sleep. On 21 February they were at 48.50° S, 24.55° E. On 22 February they were at 49° S, 32.6° E.

On 24 February John and the passengers again experienced the terrors of the Southern Ocean. John states: "The wind & sea were fearful last night. I lay in my berth listening to the roaring & dashing of waves up against the ship sides & the whistling of the wind through the rigging but I got tired & fell asleep at last."

Two days later on 26 February there was an eerie discovery:

"Strong wind all day but not very favourable. At about ½ past 9 tonight the sailor on the lookout or watch saw something a short distance ahead of the ship. He watched it till it came close to the side of the ship & he then discovered it to be a boat. According to the man's account (& another one who saw it) there was something (or somebody perhaps) laying at the bottom. The night was very dark & before the ship could be stopped & a boat lowered the other was out of sight. Now God knows it may have been some poor shipwrecked people lying dead or too much fatigued to call out. As soon as our man saw what it was he called out "Boat ahoy" but he heard no reply."

2 March and they were at 48° S, 64.10° E, and 4400 miles from New Zealand. On 4 March they saw several whales and were at 47.27° S, 72.4° E, travelling very fast. On 8 March they were at 47° S, 97.17° E. They had sailed 1400 miles in a week. Very fast. On 13 March they were opposite Cape Leuwin South Australia at 47° S, 116.10° E.

On 14 March the huge sea broke over the bulwarks and rushed down the main hatchway flooding everyone below. Boxes were "swimming about in glorious style." 46.27° S, 122.14° E.

On 18 March the sailors started cleaning and scraping as the voyage was soon ending. On 22 March they caught a small shark.

On 22 or[64] 23 March they signalled the *Dunphaile Castle* bound from London to Sydney at Lat 46° S., Long 146° E.[64] They learnt from this ship that Prince Albert had died on 13 December but no one believed this news. They were at 147.36 E. The next day they saw several large whales and a large steamer, which was the *Australian Mail*.

The night of 26 March was a night that John would never forget. It was cloudy all day with a strong contrary wind. At dusk the wind got stronger and from 8pm there was a "fearful storm" with scary lightning and thunder and squalls. One such squall sent the ship right over on its side and the man at the wheel suddenly had no control over the ship at all until an extra man helped him. Sails and booms were taken by the wind and down below everything not tied down was moving all over the place in a stream of water from the rain and breaking sea coming down the two hatchways.

Children were thrown out of bed and were screaming and crying. Some women were crying and some fainted. John helped haul ropes and he was "blundering up ladders" and hurting himself, but he didn't mind as the excitement was "so great." At midnight things started to settle. On 27 March they were at 42.6° S, 157.40° E and the weather fine and on 29 March everyone on board was getting tired of the voyage and bets were made on when they would get to New Zealand.

They had two or three days of terrible weather and then on 1 April saw two whaling ships. On 3 April, nine men took turns to climb up the rigging and strain their eyes to see land. They didn't see it though. They were at 170.35° E. John stayed up to try and see land but ended up going to bed. But just has he was going to sleep he heard a sailor call "Land oh." John jumped out of bed, jumped into his breeches and got on deck. He saw three huge rocks called the Three Kings at the North of New Zealand. Nearly every passenger got on deck to see them.

On 4 April John saw land:

"Up at daylight on purpose to get a sight at NZ. There was plenty of land – Islands on both sides of us & most dreary desolate looking patches they were. In the afternoon a strong head wind sprung up & drove us out to sea again & once more out of sight of land."

On 6 April they were becalmed and the Captain went over to a ship called Kate and got some newspapers. They learned that Prince Albert *had* actually died. Everyone started writing letters as they discovered the mail for England left Auckland soon and they wanted to arrive just before in order to send letters home.

On 7 April they arrived in Auckland:

"Went up during the night as far as we could & then signalled for a pilot. One came on board at daylight & by 7 o'clock we sighted the city of Auckland. As soon as the anchor was cast the passengers' friends came off

& then there was most affecting scenes. Husbands meeting wifes [sic] & wives meeting husbands, children meeting parents, brothers meeting sisters etc etc."

John stayed on board another night with only two other families and there was a huge gale that swamped some boats and smashed others, the worst wind at Auckland in 12 years.

John's final words are telling:

"And so finished the voyage. On the whole I think I may say I enjoyed it but I confess I began to get tired of it for being at sea there is no variety – all such a sameness & seldom seeing anything but sky & water a person may soon get tired of being on the "Mighty Ocean" & more particularly if on board such a ship as the *Cashmere*. John J Wilson"[63]

John James Wilson talked about his birds in the newspaper many years later and commented that the arrival of this particular load of birds on the *Cashmere* was the first lot dispatched to Auckland. They were sent from the Zoological Gardens at Regents Park, London for the New Zealand Government. The birds that survived were released on Kawau Island after being kept in aviaries at Government House to allow them recovery time after the voyage. The small birds became pests to farmers in New Zealand years later, but at the time people wanted to see their favourite birds from their homeland and thought they were doing a good thing. John James Wilson had years of being careful to admit that he was "the party to introduce them."

The voyage in general was uneventful with fine weather most of the passage. It took 113 days due to the light winds and calms.[65] As well as the birds there was a large and general cargo on board and a manifest. There were also about 90 passengers on board.[62]

The *Cashmere* arrived "trim and clean" and the passengers appeared "healthy and satisfied."[62]

The papers stated: "This old-established and favorite Auckland trader comes into port in her wonted trim and creditable condition, the passengers, as usual, being highly gratified with the kindly courtesy of their captain, to whom they have presented a befitting testimonial of esteem."[65]

WE the Undersigned passengers on board the Ship 'Cashmere,' Charles Gibbs Petherbridge, Commander, hereby express our unqualified approbation of the conduct of our Cook, Benjamin Thomas Hughes, we having no cause of complaint whatever from the ninth day of December, one thousand eight hundred and sixty one, to this date.

J. H. Hanson	Mary Redshaw
Ellen Hanson	Clements Jones
D. Shannon	Susan Bealys
Anne Shannon	Mary Streeter
W. J. Miller, and Wife	Mary Dooley
F. Milbourne, and Wife	Joseph Redshaw
M. Stewart, and Wife	James Carr
J. Dean	Alex. Fraser
S. Dean	Edwin Banbury
C. E. N. Bolton	Thomas Carr
Charlotte Cooper	John Redshaw
Charles Cooper	Emma Redshaw
Andrew Lumsden	Alice Redshaw
John Banbury	James East
William H. Bolton	A. T. McLaughlin
W. Edwards	William Lloyd
John J. Wilson	John Fredk. Clark
Eliza Blakley	Alfred Sayer
Anne Carr	James Whyte
Mary Jane Hicks	Betsy Whyte
Maria Walton	M. A. Wilkes
Johanna Booly	

April 7th, 1862.

Daily Southern Cross 11 April 1862

Pakeha's Birds

There was an excellent article published about the birds on the *Cashmere* in 1926 which explains more about what was involved with caring for them on board the ship and how many survived.

"Pakeha's Birds.

How They Came To N.Z.

Good Settlers.

The Feathered Choir.

Folk who glory in the out of doors in this temperate and kindly climate seldom reflect that there was a time when the lark, with its trilling welcome to the midday sun, and the pert sparrow, of whose numbers Providence keeps special tally, were not numbered among the feathered inhabitants of New Zealand. The first of the emigrants who came here, lacking the knowledge gained by the earlier missionary settlers, thought that there were few, if any, singing birds in the country; they guessed that the natives very likely ate some kinds of birds, but that there were any game birds worthy of a white man was most unlikely. The "feathered choir" whose melody at daybreak has charmed so many was not to be heard on the semidevastated ridges fronting the Waitemata. The red-billed "pukaki," as he was inelegantly called, and the mutton bird, with the aroma of its finny diet, did not appeal to persons nurtured on mildewed game in the Old Lands. The tender pigeon was a food that the Maori did not care to share with the newly arrived pakeha, to whom he was ready to sell pork and onions. The missionaries had brought fruits and flowers of different kinds to New Zealand, and the feathered natives, like the tattooed ones, had learned to appreciate their values.

Blackbirds

In 1861 the Government of the day yielded to some popular clamour to introduce the birds of the Old Lands, to give a more homelike air to the colonies in this new land as well as to fulfil the more utilitarian purpose of varying the menu. Support for the idea came from a successful effort at bird colonisation in Australia, where in ISSS the commoner varieties of Old Country birds had been "settled."

First Bird Passengers. So it came to pass that on December 9, 1861, the ship *Cashmere*, which cleared St. Katherine's Docks, carried 81 cages of singing arid game birds destined to be domiciled on the farther side of the globe in New Zealand. The prisoners had been collected under the direction of Mr, Bartlett, of the London Zoological Gardens, at the solicitation of the N.Z. Government agent, Mr. Morrison. Mr. Bartlett had previously superintended the migrating of the birds to Australia.

The bird passengers were:—

The No. Shipped.	The No. Arrived.
9 partridges	4
2 pheasants	—
12 blackbirds	10
13 thrushes	11
12 larks	10
8 goldfinches	4
8 bullfinches	3
9 linnets	6
16 chaffinches	6
18 sparrows	7
12 starlings	9
2 Canadian geese	2
4 barnacle geese	4
12 teal	11
12 widgeon	1
147	88

All circumstances considered, the mortality was not heavy; the shipboard arrangements were under the care of Mr. John Wilson, whose brother was superintendent of natural history at the Crystal Palace. The ship, which left the docks on December, did not reach Auckland until April 8, and had a severe buffeting by storms in the Bay of Biscay.

Problem of Feeding. The problem of feeding the bird travellers was of considerable complexity. The many varieties of the birds meant an almost equal variety in food supplies. Fresh food, as such, would not be procurable. Moreover, the long confinement would mean that overfed birds would succumb. The food supplies carried, for the emigrants included German paste, preserved liver, preserved fruits and vegetables, biscuit, rice, potatoes, eggs, seeds of wheat, oats, barley, hemp and flax. Ten quarts of water per diem were allocated for the needs of the feathered population in the cages. Grass seed had been grown in little boxed plots to be ready for the trip to give something like real surroundings to the prisoners. Special arrangements had to be made for the web-footed birds. Arrived at Auckland, the consignment was warmly welcomed, and hundreds of people went to the wharf to view the new arrivals who had so well borne the trials of the journey out, and whose presence recalled so many memories of life in the lands 12,000 weary miles distant. The birds were liberated on the properties of people who had volunteered to look after them. A pair of the sparrows was kept in a cage in a grocer's shop on Victoria Road, Devonport, and the youngsters of the time, some of whom were approaching their twenties, were, vastly interested in them. Most of this first migration, of the pakeha's birds seem to have prospered and to have developed into good settlers. Other migrations have occurred since, and the descendants of the firstcomers have worked their way all over New Zealand, and have found it, as the pakeha did, "God's Own Country.""[66]

1863 Voyage to Nelson

3 July 1863 – 14 October 1863

The *Cashmere* left London on 3 July 1863 and arrived at Nelson on 14 October 1863. Captain Barnett was in charge and he was already well known to those living in Nelson. It was not a fast voyage but was "a very pleasant passage." The passengers on board spoke highly of Captain Barnett's conduct and it was noted that he had received praise like this every time he had sailed to Nelson. He had "excellent seamanship and strict discipline." The *Cashmere* did not sight land after leaving England until her arrival at Nelson making it a fairly tedious journey.[67]

WOOL, &c.

Notice to Shippers.

THE ship *CASHMERE* may be expected from Nelson in about 14 days, and can receive on freight Wool or other cargo, *via* Nelson to London.
For rates of freight and other information apply to
        CHARLES BROWN, agent.
Beach Office, 4th November, 1863.

SHORTLY expected direct from England, per CASHMERE—
BRANDY
PORT WINE
Old Jamaica RUM of the best quality
        WM. DEVENISH.
Nov 7, 1863.

14 November 1863
Taranaki Herald

The ship was to be towed inside the harbour on 16 October 1863 to be berthed at once for unloading.[68]

There was some wayward crew on board the ship on this voyage. Edward Bull, James Farmer, John Hutton, Vernon Costello and Joseph Prophett, seamen from the ship *Cashmere* were all charged with desertion and were each sentenced to two months imprisonment, with hard labour.[69]

On 29 November the *Cashmere* left Nelson for New Plymouth. The ship arrived on 1 December. On 4 December the *Cashmere* had to put out to sea and did not return until 6 December. On Tuesday 8 December after discharging the cargo they took on 28 bales of wool for London. She sailed for Nelson and it was blowing strongly from the S.W. On Wednesday 9 December at 2.15 am while the jib was being stowed the foot rope parted and sailor Thomas Lang Harry fell into the sea. It was a very dark night and the sea was heavy. The life boat was lowered almost to the water but there were only two people who offered to help save Thomas, being Mr Berriman, second mate and Edward Buckingham, able bodied seaman. After waiting 25 minutes for a crew and the life boat being stove in after beating against the side of the vessel in the rough sea. Captain Barnett had to reluctantly continue his voyage to Nelson where he arrived on Friday afternoon 11 December. Poor Thomas was lost to the ocean. Thomas's brother had been drowned in the same circumstances from the ship *Edward Thornhill* on a journey from England to Nelson. They were sons of a Wesleyan Minister of St Ives.[70]

PER CASHMERE.

THE following choice WINES received, *via* London, from one of the most distinguished Houses in Portugal:—

8 quarter-casks
5 octaves   } Port—*El duque de Porto*
3   „   Bucellas—*del Rey Don Fernando*
2   „   particular Madeira—*de la quinta de Nuestra Señora de la misericordia.*

4119   JOHN BEIT.

RECEIVED PER CASHMERE.

92 FIVE-GALLON TINS PRICE'S PHOTOGENE OIL, which is warranted inexplosive, and not more inflammable than Colza.

4120   JOHN BEIT.

---

17 October 1863, Nelson Examiner and NZ Chronicle

Another Naughty Crew Member

One of the crew of the *Cashmere*, named Bowie, tried to desert the ship and was sentenced to working on a road gang on the Wakapuaka Road. He then escaped the road gang by running off into the bush. He had asked to get a drink of water and then ran off, the constable in charge firing his rifle after him but missed. He was not found![71]

The Death of a Surgeon

After ship's surgeon Mr Bloor went onshore from the *Cashmere*, he suffered a tragic accidental death. The following story was published in the newspapers:

"ACCIDENTAL DEATH OF MR. BLOOR, LATE SURGEON OF THE *CASHMERE*

On Thursday last, 14th inst., Mr. John Talberer Bloor, who came out from England to Nelson as surgeon of the ship *Cashmere,* met his death by drowning in the river Wairau, at Rainbow Valley, about 70 miles up the country from Nelson. An examination into the cause and manner of the death was held by Mr. Poynter at the Court House, Nelson, on Saturday, it being impossible to hold a coroner's inquest in the district, where the distances between the residents are so great, and so very few people living in a wide circuit of many miles. Fiven, the man who found the body of the deceased, being sworn, deposed as follows

"I am manager of Mr. Schroder's station, at Rainbow Valley, about 20 miles from the Top House, up the Wairau Gorge. The deceased came to my house on Thursday morning last about half-past nine. I never saw him before that time. He told me he had come last from Top House, and was on his way to the Clarence Valley. I did not know his name. He did not tell it to me. He asked for a drink of milk and water. I offered to make him some tea, which he refused. He had on a black cloth coat, which was all over dirt on the back, as if he had been lying on it. He told me he had come from the Top House that morning. I thought him a little deranged, as I knew he could not have done so. He enquired how far it was to White's I told him eight miles. He said he should go there and back that day if I would give him a bed at night, which I told him I would do. He asked if I had any grog, and I told him I had none. He then had a drink of water, and started, crossed the river all right, and went up the Gorge. About twelve o'clock that day Mr. White's man came down with two pack horses. I asked him if he had met a man on the road. He said no, but that there was a man knocking about on the other side of the river. I saw him on the other side; he coo-eeyed, and waved his hand to me. I told a lad at the station named George Nicol to get the horse and go for him. He did so but instead of coming back to us, the two went up the Gorge towards White's. The boy returned some time afterwards, and said he had put him all right on the track. About five o'clock the man came back again to the river, and coo-eeyed again. I told the boy to get the horse and fetch him; I went to chop some wood to make some tea for him by the time he got in. The boy went across and came back, saying he could not find the man. This was not above a quarter of an hour from the time he had coo-eeyed. I told the boy he could not be far, and I went back myself to find him. When I got to the river I found him in the middle of the ford, quite dead. There was a foot of running water at the place where he was. This was about ten chains below where I had seen him when he coo-eeyed. He was lying face downwards in the water, and his body was not quite covered. I called to the boy to assist me, and got him out and covered him over with sacks. I examined the breast pocket of his coat, and found the pocket book produced. That was the way I found his name. I came direct into town to report his death. The river was quite low at the time. It was quite safe to cross where he was when he coo-eeyed. A boy could cross there."

According to further information which we have received, it appears that the deceased had left Rolson to go, as he had stated, to Mr. Saxton's station on the Clarence Valley. He had gone, it is believed, from Nelson to Wakefield by the van on Monday, and had reached Macfarlane's house, about 17 miles further, the same day. He left Macfarlane's on Tuesday, and reached the Top House the same day. This he left on Wednesday, and had probably been out all night in the bush, and from lack of food (for he ate nothing at any of the places he called at and only had some grog at each) he had got bewildered and forgot the time. It is supposed that in attempting to cross the river at the ford, he had grown giddy, partly from exhaustion and partly from the dizzying effect of the running water—which, it is well known, produces great giddiness if a person crossing looks at it in the passage instead of keeping the eye on the opposite bank—and had fallen forward on his face in the position in which he was found, and from weakness had been unable to rise again. Dr. Bloor, who held a regular diploma and had, we understand, been in practice in England, appeared to be about thirty-two or thirty-three years of age. He was engaged by Messrs, Shaw, Saville, and Co. to return to England in the *Cashmere*.

We have also learned that the only article produced to the Magistrate as being found on the body was the pocket book of the deceased, in which were numerous letters and other documents. Other things were found but Fivan, the witness who picked the man out of the water, labors under the erroneous notion that he is entitled to all the property found on the body; and has, we believe, even gone the length of selling, or bargaining for the sale of, a valuable brooch which was in Dr. Bloor's possession when he lost his life. What he may have made of any other articles is not known. We could hardly have supposed that any one could imagine that the finder of a dead body is entitled to the property upon it. The finder has no more right to it than he has to the watch or purse of a man he may find asleep in the bush. The articles in cases of the kind ought to be delivered to the Registrar of Intestate Estates Court, and disposed of by him for behalf of the next of kin according to law. The person who helps himself to a dead man's property becomes liable to a criminal prosecution. [72]

Final Departure of the *Cashmere*

The *Cashmere* left Nelson for London on about 11 March 1864 after being loaded up with wool for the return journey. It never did come back to New Zealand, this being her final journey to the colony. The ship was loaded up with 96,570 lbs. of wool from Nelson alone as well as a lot of other wool,[73] totalling 1658 bales of wool, 10 bales of skins, 336 tons of chrome ore and a lot of plumbago. The total value of the cargo was 85,935 pounds. She was so "deeply laden" that she "could scarcely cross the bar safely before Monday." Usually ships would go to Port Underwood to load the wool, but not the *Cashmere* which loaded everything at Nelson.[74]

Cashmere Passengers

Cashmere Passengers

The following is a selection of passengers that came to New Zealand on the *Cashmere* journeys. It is by no means complete, the *Cashmere* transporting close to 900 passengers in her career as an immigrant ship.

Banbury

John Banbury was born in Burford, Oxfordshire and travelled on the *Cashmere* in 1861. He stayed in Auckland a short time before chasing gold at Coromandel where he saw the opening of the first gold rush. He didn't see immediate wealth so went to Dunedin and travelled to Gabriel's Gully but it was too cold for him so he went back to Auckland! In 1863 war broke out in the Waikato and John Banbury became very involved in the wars and received the Queen's Medal at the close of the campaign. He became a commercial traveller once back in Auckland and had to travel by Maori tracks or over the sea. He bought land at Ponsonby in 1864, then known as "Dedwood" and built a house there. He married in 1866 and established a small Sunday School which later turned into St John's Methodist Church. He died in 1936 aged 92.[75]

Bolton

Mr. T. Bolton

Thomas Bolton was born in Gloucestershire, England in 1849 and came to the New Zealand on the *Cashmere* in 1855 with his parents. He grew up on his father's farm in Riccarton and when aged 20 years he leased a farm from Captain Halkett in the Kimberley district. He bought part of Westington Farm, Kirwee in 1879 and built it up to 590 acres. He reared fat lambs for the export trade and bred crossbred ewes and Shropshire rams for the purpose. He had a good seven room house and out buildings, an orchard, garden and plantations as well as twelve paddocks. He served on the school committee and was a member of the Courtenay A and P Association and exhibited successfully. He married Miss Griffiths in 1874 who died in 1877 leaving three daughters. He then married Miss Kirk in 1880 and they had one daughter.[76]

Brabant

Harry Stamforth Brabant was the son of William Hugh Brabant of London. He came to New Zealand in the *Cashmere* in 1863. He served in the Maori Wars and later settled at Waipa. In 1869 he married to Miss Graham, daughter of James Graham and in 1882 they went to live in Tauranga where Harry's brother was Stipendiary Magistrate. He farmed at Otumoetai and then moved to Devonport and then Remuera. When Harry died in 1926, he left four sons and six daughters to mourn his loss.[77]

Bray

Mrs E. A. Bray was born in Southampton, England in 1840, the daughter of Henry Smith of Mount Eden, Auckland and came to New Zealand by the *Cashmere* in 1854. Her husband was James Bray who was accidentally drowned in the Wairoa River. She lived in Auckland for 70 years and died in 1925 leaving seven daughters and two sons as well as 20 grandchildren and one great grandchild.[78]

Bristow

Richard Bristow was born in Lincolnshire in 1838, and came to Lyttelton on the ship *Cashmere* in 1861. He lived in Kaiapoi before moving to Gebbie's Valley, working with timber in both places. In 1867 he purchased land at Amberley when the town was just being established. When he died in 1914 he left a widow and a family to mourn his loss.[79]

Compton

Miss Elizabeth Jane Compton came to Lyttelton on the *Cashmere* in 1859 and lived in Christchurch until 1878. She then moved to Ashburton. Her sister was Mrs Fooks with whom she lived with until her death in 1904 aged 72. She was a member of St. Stephen's Church and worked hard there in the choir and teaching Sunday School.[80]

Cowie

Mr and Mrs Cowie were apparently passengers on the Cashmere in 1851 although are not listed on the passenger list. Their son, William Cowie was born at Parnell, Auckland. He was employed at the timber mills at Mercury Bay where he met his wife, the daughter of the a chieftainess of the Ngati Awa tribe. He took up farming in the district and retired to Auckland. When he died in 1945 he was survived by his wife, 1 son, 2 daughters and 8 grandchildren. Two sons were killed in the Great War.[81]

Cox

William and Arabella Cox came out to New Zealand on the ship *Cashmere* in 1859. Mr Cox was the first schoolmaster at Riccarton. They both taught at the public school at Rakaia and then had a general store. They attended St. Mark's Church. Arabella died in 1899 leaving a daughter and two sons.[82]

Craighead

John Craighead came to Lyttelton in 1859 in the *Cashmere* with his wife and five children. They settled at Prebbleton but in 1865 moved to Russell's Flat, Canterbury, where John bought a farm. He never resided permanently on it, however. He died at Prebbleton in 1884 leaving a family of seven sons and one daughter.[83]

Mr. D. Craighead

David Craighead, son of John Craighead settled in Russell's Flat in 1874 and started farming. In 1881 he bought a property in the area which consisted of 152 acres of land. He farmed sheep and grew grain. He was a shareholder in many farming companies and was director and chairman of the Malvern Saleyards Company. He was a member of the Russell's Flat school committee. He married a daughter of Mr. David Lamb of Christchurch and they had two sons and one daughter.[84]

Elder

Peter Elder was born at Wick, Caithness, Scotland and came to Lyttelton by the ship *Cashmere* in 1859. He first worked for Mr. G. H. Moore of Glenmark and after living on the estate for some years entered into a partnership with his brother Hugh Elder. They became stock dealers between Canterbury and the West Coast for about fourteen years, during the gold digging days. After giving up the business he farmed at Clarkville, Kaiapoi for ten years. He was then appointed assistant yardman for the Canterbury Saleyards Company, a job which he held for thirty-two years, until his death in 1913. He acted as sheep and sheep-dog judge at agricultural shows and was one of the founders of the Papanui ploughing matches. He was a quiet unassuming man with many friends.[85]

Eustace

Alfred Eustace arrived in Auckland in 1857 on the *Cashmere*. He opened one of the first butcher's shops in Auckland and served in the Maori War. He died in 1920 leaving one son and three daughters.[86]

Ferguson

John Ferguson was born in Northern Ireland and travelled to New Zealand on the *Cashmere* in 1854. He lived his whole life in the East Tamaki district where he was greatly respected. He left behind a widow, one son and five daughters when he died in 1901.[87]

Fleming

Mrs Samuel Fleming arrived on the *Cashmere* in 1851 and lived to be 90, dying in 1913. She was the sister of Rev Thomas Hamer who was also on the ship. She was an original member of the Independent Church in Albert Street where the Rev. Thomas Hamer was pastor for many years. When she died at her residence in Takapuna, she was survived by her son Mr J Fleming and a married daughter.[88]

Foster

Mrs Amelia Foster (need Wells) died in 1925 aged 92. She travelled to Lyttelton with her parents on the *Cashmere* in 1855. She married Captain J. Foster and lived most of her life at Okain's Bay as well as Lyttelton. She was a good church woman and widely read. She used to reminisce on the early days of New Zealand. When she died she left a family of eleven, three daughters and six sons.[89]

Gillatt

Joseph Robinson Gillatt was born in Lincolnshire, England in 1837. He was brought up with farming life and came to Lyttelton via Port Chalmers on the ship *Cashmere* in 1861. He lived on Banks Peninsula for sixteen years then moved to South Canterbury where he leased the "Stumps Farm" at Orari. He then bought 460 acres at Seadown. He married in Lincolnshire and they had five children.[90]

Gray

James Gray was born near Skipton, Yorkshire, England in 1826. He was brought up as a farmer and followed this profession before travelling to Lyttelton, by the ship *Cashmere*, in about 1864. He settled almost immediately in the East Eyreton district, and about two years afterwards purchased his first section of fifty acres of land, which he subsequently increased to seventy acres. James married the daughter of Mr H. Laytham of York in 1855. James died in 1890, leaving three daughters and a widow.[91]

Gunn

David Gunn was born in Caithness-shire, Scotland in 1858, the son of Mr John Gunn and was brought out to Lyttelton, New Zealand on the *Cashmere* in 1859. His parents settled in Christchurch and David was educated at the High School and then brought up on his father's farm at Templeton. In 1879 he took up Hayfield Farm in Hook which was 124 acres and another farm of 310 acres, used for grazing. He was a member of the Waituna School Committee and a member of the Foresters' Court, Waimate. In 1887 he married a daughter of Mr. Donald Gunn of the Hook and they had two sons and three daughters.[92]

Hall

Mrs Robert Hall was the sister of Rev John Macky, who was minister of the Presbyterian Church, Otahuhu for many years. She came to New Zealand on the *Cashmere* in 1854. She lived on the land in the South Island with her husband for many years and experienced the hard early years of colonial life. She had a sweet nature which was much loved. When she died at her residence at One Tree Hill, aged 78 years in 1916, she was survived by her husband, five sons and three daughters.[93]

Hamer

Rev. Thomas Hamer, from Lancashire, arrived on the *Cashmere* in 1851 after being sent out by the London Mission Society so that he could found an Independent Church in Auckland. However, Dr. Alex McDonald, beat him to it! Rev. Hamer started preaching in the Oddfellows' Hall on Queen Street, Auckland. He then purchased a three room cottage in Albert Street. He moved, four years before his death, to Wellington where his son lived. When he died in 1899, he had one son and two daughters living.[94]

Hamerton

Lewis Alexander Hamerton came to New Plymouth on the *Cashmere* in 1854, with his mother, three brothers and two sisters, all of which predeceased him, except his brother Thomas. Lewis was 82 when he died in 1914. He was managing clerk to several firms and then went into the farming industry. He was survived by a wife, eight daughters and one son.[95]

Thomas Edward Hamerton, brother of Lewis, died in 1919. He was born at Fernley, Lancashire, England. He lived in New Plymouth for many years and then moved to Patea in 1881. Three years later he bought the *Patea Mail* which turned into the *Patea Press*. He ran it until 1901 when he went to Inglewood and took over the *Record*. He was senior partner of the firm and editor of the *Record* at the time of his death. He left a family of four sons and four daughters to mourn his loss.[96]

Captain Robert Chisenhall Hamerton was born at the Hollins, Lancashire, England, and educated at the Queen Elizabeth Grammar School, Yorkshire. He arrived in New Zealand by the *Cashmere* in 1854, and farmed on his father's farm before joining the Taranaki Militia as an officer. He fought in the Maori Wars and was wounded at the battle of Waireka. He received the N.Z. war medal for his services.

Captain R. C. Hamerton

After the Maori wars he entered the Civil Service, and in 1871 was appointed Registrar of the Supreme Court in Wellington. He was a Freemason, musician and member of St. Mark's Church where he played the organ. He married Miss A. Parris.[97]

Hawley

Mrs F. G. Hawley arrived on the ship *Cashmere* in October 1859 with her husband and infant son. A year later they were appointed master and mistress of St. Michael's Church school by Bishop Harper which they held until 1870. They then opened a private school. When she died in 1912 aged 82 she left two sons and seven grandchildren.[98]

Henderson

Mrs David Henderson arrived with her husband and one son in Auckland by the ship *Cashmere* in 1851. After a few years in New Zealand they visited several other colonies (including Melbourne, Adelaide and Sydney[99]), but returned to Auckland in 1861. They lived for several years at Henderson's Mill but in 1868 she moved to Thames with her family. She was known as a kind-hearted, generous woman. She died suddenly of heart failure on the verandah of her house. She exclaimed "I believe I am dying," and died a few moments after a doctor arrived. She left behind a large grown up family and 19 grandchildren.[100]

Heyward

Mrs Heyward arrived on the *Cashmere* and resided at Kaiapoi Island for the rest of her life. She was married to James Heyward. She died in 1897 at an "advanced age."[101]

Hill

Mr W. Shirley Hill and his father Henry Hill arriving in the *Cashmere* in 1853. He entered the Customs Department and worked his way up to chief clerkship. He then set up his own business and at his death controlled one of the largest businesses of any kind in Auckland. He was a devoted churchman. He had a weak heart and had a sudden seizure at a meeting. A doctor was sent for but he died a few minutes later aged 73. He left a wife and grown up family.[102]

Ivory

William Emms Ivory was the oldest inhabitant of the Rangiora district when he died in 1911 at the age of 94. He was from Norwich, England and came to Lyttelton in the *Cashmere* in 1855.

He was trained as a gardener in his early life. He settled almost immediately at Rangiora, at first being employed by Mr Hamilton Ward and he claimed to have erected the first workman's cottage. He assisted to sow and reap the first crop of wheat on the land, part of which is now King Street. He bought his own land on the margin of the large native forest of about 3000 acres that extended from Rangiora to Kaiapoi and put it into tillage and grew a record crop of wheat. William imported stocks of seeds and plants and established a nursery for fruit and other trees. He was an expert in horticulture. He wasn't interested in public life but was a pastor of the Baptist church when it was first opened in 1862. When he died he left several children. He had married twice, outliving both wives.[103]

Jackson

Joseph Jackson was a native of Sussex, England and arrived in Lyttelton in the *Cashmere* in 1855. He was a carpenter near Christchurch for 11 years before moving to Rangiora and taking up a farm at Fernside. He was a member of the school committee and had an interest in public affairs. On his death in 1909 he left behind a widow, four sons and one daughter.[104]

Jonas

Moss Jonas was born at Brighton, England in April 1839 and worked on river steamboats in London at the age of thirteen. He came to Port Chalmers in February 1860 on the *Cashmere* and then spent a few years in Christchurch. He settled in Timaru in 1868 and began a furniture and crockery business and then auctioneering. He did a tour of Canada, America and other parts of the world which took five years. At the Melbourne Exhibition of 1888 he was one of the commissioners representing the New Zealand Government. He served on the Timaru Borough Council for seventeen years and became Mayor of Timaru. He was also a member of the Harbour Board for sixteen years. He married in May 1871 to a daughter of the late Mr Philip Symondson of London and they had five sons and three daughters.[105] He died in 1907 while playing cards with members of his family. He fell back, expiring at once.[106]

Lynds

William Lynds was born in Kent, England and came to New Zealand with his wife and family in 1857 on the ship *Cashmere*. He was a "sturdy pioneer" and him and his wife had reared a family of 12, seven of whom were left to mourn his death in 1902. His wife was also still alive. They celebrated their diamond wedding not long before his death.[107]

Martin

Albin Martin was born in about 1812 or 1813 in Dorsetshire, England. He was an artist and farmer and travelled to New Zealand with his wife Jemima and six children in 1851 and wrote a diary while on board. He had a massive attack of gout whilst on the ship and had to be carried to their first house in Auckland. After going to the hot pools at Waiwera he recovered and soon started farming at Pakuranga Stream.

In 1865 he had a series of sketches of the Coromandel gold mining district published in the *Illustrated London News*.

He died in 1888 leaving a wife and eight children to mourn his loss.[108]

McCall

Mr and Mrs C. M. McCall came out to New Zealand on the *Cashmere* in 1853 to assist with missionary work amongst the Maori with Bishop William Williams. Mrs McCall took on the job of assistant instructor at the Thames Mission Station under Rev. Lanfear. She stayed in the position until the Maori War started. She lived in Thames for 34 years and died in 1899 leaving a grown family of two sons and two daughters.[109] The McCall's son, William R. McCall was believed to be the first white child born in the Thames District and the Maori took a great interest in him, one chief even offering to buy him. William grew up to farm in the Coromandel district and then moved to Auckland. He died in 1937 and was survived by his wife, a daughters with another son killed in the Great War.[110]

Okey

Edward Okey was born in Stroud, Gloucestershire and learnt the trade of house decorating. He came to New Zealand in 1857 on the *Cashmere* and settled in New Plymouth. He worked in sawmilling until troubles with the Maori forced him to move to town where he enrolled himself in the militia. After war he took up farming but gave that up and started a painting and house decorating business in New Plymouth. He died in 1910, aged 82, and one of his sons was an M.P for Taranaki.[111]

Pearce

William Pearce was born in 1831 in Camberwell, London, England. His father was Henry Pearce, a wine cooper or cellar man and his mother was Mary Lowe. William, who was a barrister's clerk in Surrey, married Jane Fogden at St Paul's, Bermondsey, Surrey on 26-02-1854. William came out to New Zealand on the *Cashmere* in 1859 captained by John Byron and was the schoolmaster on board the ship.

Jane and three young Pearce children must have come out to New Zealand later (about 1862). So William Pearce started his new life in New Zealand without his family. He is listed in the Canterbury Militia List (a list of able men for local defence) for the year ending 31-03-1861 as a storeman living in Dublin Street, Lyttelton.

William was then chosen as Inspector of Nuisances out of 46 applicants after John Coker resigned on 20-06-1863. William was assaulted in the course of his duties and the defendant W. H. McKellow was fined 2 pounds by C. C. Bowen on 11-07-1867. The defendant said: "in the heat of passion, he had committed the offence with which he was charged. His Worship said that public servants must be protected in the execution of their duty."

William was also Inspector of Hackney Carriages and in November 1872, prosecuted a cabman for not displaying a table of fares in his cab. He also gave evidence in a case concerning a hackney carriage by-law in March 1874. William's job must have made him one of the most hated men in Christchurch being similar to a council inspector and traffic warden all in one.

William Pearce's first wife Jane Fogden died on 16-10-1869 aged 38 years. She is buried in the Barbadoes Street cemetery. Jane and William had seven children including five boys and two girls.

His second wife was Elizabeth Kelly née Nancarrow (widow of Richard Seymour Kelly who died 25-10-1873). William and Elizabeth married on 14-11-1875 at St. Luke's, Christchurch. They had two girls.

William owned a property on London Street, Richmond, that was part rural section 41 and was freehold. William died on 29-08-1900 aged 69 at London Street, Richmond, Christchurch and is buried in the Barbadoes Street Cemetery with his second wife Elizabeth who died on 15-09-1924 aged 86.[112]

Pearson

William Pearson was born in Yorkshire, England in 1838 and came to Lyttelton on the *Cashmere* in 1859. He went to Springs Station and then helped to survey land around Christchurch. He later went to Mount Somers station and when the Springs estate was subdivided, William sold some land which he had bought at Rolleston and purchased a property at Lincoln. The land was in its wild native state, partly cover by water and overgrown with flax. He turned it into productive farmland. William was churchwarden for several years. He died in 1886 leaving a widow, four sons and one daughter. His eldest son John Pearson worked for the Central Dairy Company, son Robert W. Pearson was a farmer and sons George and Herbert Pearson resided on the family estate. Mrs Pearson was from Tipperary, Ireland and came to New Zealand on the *Zealandia* in 1862. She married William Pearson in 1865.[113]

Prins

Henry Horsford Prins was born Colombo, Ceylon to Dr John Theobald Prins who held a high position in the Indian Army and who married in India. Henry got some medical experience in England and then came to Lyttelton on the *Cashmere* in 1859 as the surgeon. He started a practice in Christchurch and eventually took charge of Christchurch Hospital which was in a bad state. After organising the hospital he was given control of the all the public institutions under the Provincial Government, including the Lunatic Asylum, Police Department etc. He did this job for three years and then resigned, returning to his practice. He was one of the founders of the Christchurch Horticultural Society and a member of the Canterbury Acclimatisation Society as well as other institutions. He was into racing and bred horses and was a member of the Canterbury Jockey Club. He married in 1875 to the daughter of Colonel Lean and they had two sons and six daughters. He died in 1896 and was buried in Riccarton Churchyard.[114]

Rickit

Joseph Rickit was born in England in 1852 and came to New Zealand with his parents in 1861 on the *Cashmere*. They settled at *Cashmere* and Mr Rickit, senior was one of the first butchers in that district. Mr Rickit junior joined the Armed Constabulary and later set up a store in Taupo with a partner. He also owned a bullock dray and had a transport business. In 1870 he married Taima Te Ngahue a Maori lady of high rank in the Tohurangi tribe who went through the Tarawera eruption. He died in 1926 and was survived by his wife, four sons, six daughters and 28 grandchildren.[115]

Rutherford

Mrs D. H. Rutherford was the daughter of Mr John Perry of New Plymouth. She was born in Cornwall and came to New Zealand on the *Cashmere* in 1855 or 1856 and with her parents became an early settler with many trials and challenges. She married Mr D. H. Rutherford in New Plymouth and lived at Hawera where they had to flee for a while due to the Maori Wars. Their son John was the first white child to be taken to live in the Hawera District. They lived in Turakina and then Feilding before there was a proper settlement there. She was a cheery and helpful person. She died in 1910 and left a family of four sons and nine daughters.[116]

Runciman

Elizabeth and George Runciman and their family arrived in the *Cashmere* in 1851. They settled at Papatoetoe and lived there until George died. Elizabeth then moved to town. Elizabeth died in 1887 leaving one son and four daughters behind.[117]

Schmidt

Mrs F. Schmidt came to Lyttelton in the *Cashmere* in 1855 and lived in Ashley for 35 years. She died in 1900.[118]

Scott

Walter Henry Scott was born in London in 1828 and in his youth learned the builder's trade. He arrived in New Plymouth in 1854 on the *Cashmere* and started a contracting business in Devon Street.

He joined the Taranaki militia and fought in the Maori wars. He was present at the battle of the Mahoetahi and served through the whole war, receiving the N.Z. war medal for his service. He was elected a member of the town board. He helped institute the Borough Council and was a member of that for six years. He was also a member of the Harbour Board and the school committee as well as being on the Licensing Committee.

Mr. W. H. Scott

He married his wife in 1852 in England and came to New Zealand because of her health. She died in 1892 leaving three sons and three daughters.[119]

Stanton

Joseph Stanton, of Kaiapoi had arrived in the *Cashmere* in 1854. He died in 1913. His son was Mr S. G. Stanton, postmaster at Stratford.[120]

Stapleforth

Hannah and William Stapleforth arrived in the *Cashmere* in 1855 at Lyttelton. Hannah died in 1907 and had lived in Rangiora for over 50 years. They were amongst some of the first settlers of North Canterbury. Hannah was survived by her husband three daughters, one son, twenty-two grandchildren and three great-grandchildren.[121]

One of their daughters was Mrs Hannah Stichbury (nee Stapleforth). She was born at Rangiora and lived for many years at Epsom and later Takapuna. After her husband William died in 1918 she moved to Remuera. She died in 1938 aged 82, leaving children and several grandchildren.[122]

Stokes

Thomas was born at Branston, Leicestershire, on 25 July 1830, the son of Thomas & Elizabeth Stokes (nee White). His two older half brothers were William Stokes who arrived in Canterbury with his wife and family on the *Randolph* in 1850 and John who also arrived with his wife and family on the *Caroline Agnes* in 1855. His younger brother Robert arrived later on the on the *Joseph Fletcher*. Both younger brothers arrived in Lyttelton as single men.

Before Thomas departed from England on the *Cashmere* in 1855 he had previously been apprenticed to Robert Lord who was a Carpenter & Joiner of Eaton which was several miles south of Branston, his apprenticeship commenced on 21 July 1846 and his family are still in possession of the original apprenticeship certificate.

Thomas Stokes' first marriage was to Mary Wilkinson at Holy Trinity, Avonside, on 20 August 1857 and in those days they lived in Cashel Street with their four children. He was a member of the Christchurch Militia in 1860. After Mary's death he remarried Caroline Weavers (nee Deal), a family friend, whose husband had died. Caroline had arrived in Lyttelton as a single woman on the *Egmont* in 1856. There were no children by her previous marriage and they were married at St. John's Anglican Church, Leeston on 27 December 1876. Their only child was Frank Deal Stokes born 20 February 1880 and for many years the family lived at "Koromiko Cottage", 11 Philips Street, Linwood, near Christchurch.

Thomas died 8th January 1898, aged 66 years and was buried at the Barbadoes Street Cemetery, although his name is on the family grave in the Bromley Cemetery.

Warner

Thomas Warner was born in London and took up the profession of scenic artist at Covent Garden, Vauxhall and other "noted place of amusement in his day." He came to New Zealand in the *Cashmere* in 1853 and became an old and highly-respected Auckland identity. He was one of the promoters of the first art exhibition in Auckland. He moved to Coromandel in later life and lived with his son. He had extraordinary vitality and could read extremely small type without glasses. He died at age 98 in 1899 leaving a son, grandchildren and great grandchildren behind.[123]

Watson

William Morgan Watson arrived at Lyttelton on the *Cashmere* in 1855. William was with Mr. Bray at Avonhead for a year or two and then the family settled at Spreydon where they farmed for many years. The last ten years of William's life was spent in retirement at Fendalton. He died in 1898 at the age of 69 leaving a family of five sons and five daughters.

Mr. W. M. Watson

Mr. G. Watson

One son, George Watson was born at Hull, Yorkshire and was only one when he arrived in New Zealand. He took up 70 acres in West Melton in 1870 and increased this to 1100 acres, calling it Melton Hills Farm. He was a member of the Courtenay Road Board for twelve years and was on the West Melton School Committee. He married a daughter of Mr. John Hill, one of the first settlers of West Melton and they had two sons and three daughters.[124]

Wells

Mr and Mrs Wells and 5 children came to Lyttelton in 1855. In 1924 the children had a family reunion with four of the children in their 80s, with their ages totally 338 years. Living descendants of the original immigrant couple totalled 211 in 1924 including 124 great grandchildren and 43 great great grandchildren![125]

One of the sons, Mr James Wells died at the age of 96 in 1938. He had been born on 9 March 1842 near Bexley and Eltham, West Kent, England. His family settled in Lyttelton and James got his first job at 13 years old on a back country shearing camp. There was a "carousal" and he was so frightened he ran away and walked back to Lyttelton! He then worked as a messenger boy and then butcher in Lyttelton. Once a bullock carcass fell on him and he didn't recover from the injuries for five months! He married and settled at Okains Bay and worked in a pit sawing business. He then turned to farming.[126]

Wilkinson

Thomas Merrett Wilkinson was a medical practitioner who came out to New Zealand as the ship's doctor on the *Cashmere* arriving in 1860. He then went to Melbourne but returned to Dunedin in 1862 and purchased a chemist's business in Princes Street. He was a member of the city council to which he was elected in 1868. He died at his home in Dunedin on 15 October 1899 at 75 years old and left a widow and one son.[127]

Wilson

Mr John Alexander Wilson was born in Quimper, France. He came to Auckland at one year old in the *Cashmere* in 1856 and was educated at Auckland Grammar School and St. John's College. At 18 he got a job in the Public Works Department at Wellington. He did this job most of his life until retirement. He was district engineer at Auckland after being resident engineer at Wellington. He helped construct Midland Railway in the South Island and was the first engineer in charge of the Otira section and then the Springfield end. He was also involved with constructing the Main Truck Railway in the North Island. He died in 1928 aged 72 and was survived by three daughters.[128]

Wilson

John James Wilson arrived in Auckland on the *Cashmere* in 1862. He was in charge of the English birds on board the ship. He died in 1918 at Mercury Bay and was survived by his wife, four sons and three daughters. Four of his grandchildren were on active service at the time of his death.[129]

Passenger Lists

Passenger Lists

The following lists have been transcribed directly from either original passenger lists or lists in old newspapers. Corrections were made after research was done on the passengers. The original transcriptions are in square brackets beside the correct spelling.

Cashmere Passengers 1851 to Auckland[20]

Gravesend (16 Jun 1851) to Auckland (19 Oct 1851)
Under Captain George Pearson

Bayly	Rev. George		Hamilton	Mrs Jessie
Bayly	Mrs		Hamilton	Child
Bayly	Children (3)		Henderson	Mr David
Bourke	Mrs		Henderson	Mrs
Bourke	Child		Henderson	Child
Brodie	Mr Walter		Hutchinson	Mrs
Bromley	Mr Henry		Isaacs	Miss Sarah
Bromley	Mrs		Isaacs	Mr D
Brown	Mr R.L.		Macintosh	Mrs
Campbell	Mr		Macintosh	Child
Conway	Mr		Martin	Mr
Conway	Mrs Catherine		Martin	Mrs
			Martin	Children (6)
Conway	Miss Mary		Mitchell	Mr J.
Courtney	Mr		Moyle	Mr Loftus
Courtney	Mrs		Reid	Mr Conrad
Courtney	Children (6)		Runciman	Mr B.
Cutress	George		Runciman	Walter
Cutress	Thomas		Runciman	Master
Cutress	Charles		Runciman	Mr George
Cuttress	Miss Alice		Runciman	Mrs
Cuttress	Miss Emma		Runciman	Miss
Cuttress	Miss Sophia		Runciman	Miss Elizabeth
Cuttress	Miss Charlotte			
			Runciman	Miss Jane
Cuttress	Miss H.		Runciman	Isabella
Cuttress	Miss B.		Saunders	Mr John
Doyle	Mr Thomas		Sheppard	Miss
Doyle	Son		Smith	Mr Henry
Dudley	Rev W.C.		Smith	Mrs
Ely	Mrs		Smith	Children (4)
Ford	Mr Samuel		Smithers	Mr Henry
Ford	Mrs		Smithers	Mrs
Ford	Children (5)		Smithers	Children (3)
Francis	Jane		Tiddif/Tiddy	Miss Martha
Gol(d)sborough	Miss Mary		Wadman	Mr
Graham	Mr John		Wethered	Mrs
Hamer	Rev Thomas		Wethered	Children (2)
Hamer	Miss		Williams	Mr John
Hamer	Mrs			
Hamer	Children (2)			
Hamilton	Mr James			

Cashmere Passengers 1853 to Auckland[27]

London (22 Oct 1852) to Auckland (9 May 1853)

Under Captain George Pearson

Bell	Miss
Boswell	Mr
Dalton	Miss Hannah
Danvers	Mr
Dover	W.
Jones	Miss Frances
Lanfear	Miss Emma
Nicklin	C. R.
Porter	Mr. Edward
Porter	Maria
Portous	Richard
Portous	Adelaide
Stephenson	M. A.
Tomes	Miss Anne

Tyler	C.
Tyler	H. W.
Walker	Miss Matilda
White	George
Williams	Archdeacon William
Williams	Capt W.
Williams	Hannah
Williams	Susannah
Williams	Mary Ann
Williams	Miss
Williams	Mr James
Williams	Mrs

Cashmere Passengers 1854 to New Plymouth and Auckland[39]

London (20 Apr 1854) to New Plymouth (6 Aug 1854) and Auckland (21 Aug 1854)

Under Captain George Pearson

New Plymouth Passengers	
Sealy	Dr.
Sealy	Mrs
Sealy	William
Sealy	Maude
Sealy	Alfred
Hammerton	Holden
Hammerton	Eliza
Hammerton	Eliza Jane
Hammerton	Isabella
Hammerton	Robert
Hammerton	Edward
Hammerton	Gervase
Hammerton	Gilbert
Hammerton	Emma
Hammerton	Louisa
Hammerton	Edward
Hinde	Thomas
Hinde	Mary
Artimage	E.
Carrington	C.
Carrington	Mrs.
Carrington	Jane.
Corbet	J.
Davis	Margaret

Dean	B.
Fathers	P.
Fathers	Elizabeth
Fathers	John
Hendrey	Joseph
Hendrey	Mary
Honeyban	Mary
Honnor	George
Honnor	Mary
Heaton	W.
Heaton	R.
King	J.
Kirk	W.
Mckenzie	S.
Mckenzie	C.
Scott	W.
Scott	Mary
Stutterd	J.
Stutterd	Jane
Stutterd	John
Stutterd	Benjamin
Stutterd	Edward
Stutterd	Alfred
Stutterd	Charlotte
Stutterd	Walter

Passenger Lists

Stutterd	Emily
Taylor	Amelia
Ware	G.
Shore	J.
Shore	Hannah
Ware	D.
Ware	Mary Ann

Ware	Emily
Ware	Mary Nn
Ware	George
Ware	Laura
Ware	James
Ware	Sarah

Auckland Passengers	
Macky	Rev. John
Macky	Mrs
Macky	S.
Macky	John
Macky	James
Macky	Margaret
Macky	Elizabeth
Alexander	Mrs.
Alexander	John
Alexander	Weller
Alexander	Henry
Alexander	Sarah
Motherell	Mr. S.
Motherell	Joseph
Motherell	Elizabeth
Motherell	Jane

Motherell	Sarah
Motherell	Selitia
Macky	Mr.
Macky	Mrs.
Latimer	Mr. N.
Macky	Miss
Nixon	Mrs E.
Armstage	Mr. E.
Dean	Mr. B
Dunlop	Mr. J.
Furgurson	Mr. J.
Harrison	Mr. J.
Judges	Mr. W.
Millard	Mr. F.
Macfarlane	Mr H.
Nordell	Ann
Wallace	Moses

Cashmere Passengers 1855 into Lyttelton[131]

London (2 Jul 1855) to Lyttelton (23 Oct 1855)

Name		Age	County	Occupation
Second Cabin				
Franks	Francis	27		Schoolmaster on Board
Harkins	Mr	24		Schoolmaster
	Mrs	24		Schoolmistress
Younger	Mr			Lyttelton Times[114]
Atkinson	Mr			
Brown				
Skinner	Miss			
Crompton	Miss			
Unassisted Steerage passengers				
Hunt	Mr and Mrs			Lyttelton Times[115]
McNaughten	Mrs			
Mansey	Miss			
Families & Children				
Bailey	Benjamin	38		Labourer
	Kezia	38		
Boulton	Richard	45		Labourer
	Hester	40		
	Joseph	9		
	Richard	7		
	Thomas	5		

Passenger Lists

	Elizabeth	3	
	George	1	
	Robert	Infant	
Bright	George	27	Labourer
	Harriet	33	
	Edward	3	
	George	Infant	
Brown	James	33	Labourer
	Anne	27	
	John	1	
Gerken	John	33	Labourer
	Katherine	35	
	John	6	
	Maria	3	
	Anna Maria	Infant	
Hayton	James	26	Mason
	Louisa	27	
Hill	Charles	30	Carpenter
	Mary	25	
	Lenora	2	
	Robert	Infant	
Hood	John	37	Labourer
	Emma	36	
	William	13	
	Thomas	10	
	Jane	7	
	Elizabeth	4	
	John	Infant	
Ivory	William	34	Gardener
	Betsy	34	
	John	12	
	Betsy	7	
	Priscilla	3	
	Edward	1	
Jones	Matthew	28	Labourer
	Sarah	25	
	William	1	
Laffhagen	Johann	28	Labourer
	Matthda	23	
	Henry	Infant	
May	George	25	Dairyman
	Mary	25	
	Elizabeth	3	
	Ephraim	Infant	
Orchard	Charles	27	Sawyer
	Jane	23	
	Samuel	1	
Parnham	John	25	Sawyer
	Maria	21	
	Anne	1	
Pierce	John	32	Gardener
	Eliza	28	
	Thomas	10	
	John	8	

Passenger Lists

	William	6		
	George	4		
	Eliza	2		
	Alma	Infant		
Pring	Thomas	33		Shoemaker
	Eliza	30		
	Marianne	6		
	Lydia	4		
	Thomas	2		
Ray	Simon	32		Labourer
	Mary	32		
	Robert	12		
	William	10		
	James	8		
	Rachel	6		
	John	4		
	Thomas	2		
	Adam	Infant		
Stapleforth	William	26		Farm Servant
	Hannah	21		
	Hepzibah	Infant		
Staunton	Joseph	24		Labourer
	Hanah	24		
	John	5		
	William	2		
	Sarah	Infant		
Watson	William	30		Dairyman
	Maria	32		
	Sarah	Infant		
Watson	William	25		Farm and General Servant
	Elizabeth	26		
	James	2		
	George	Infant		
Watson	Josiah	34		Dairyman
	Sarah	36		
Wells	Thomas	49		Woodsman
	Sarah	50		
	James	13		
	Edgar	10		
Werry	William	36		Labourer
	Marianne	29		
	William	Infant		
Younghusband	John	41		Printer
	Marianne	34		
	Marianne	13		
	Frederick	10		
	Clara	9		
	Emma	7		
	John	Infant		
Single Men				
Austen	John	68		Farm Labourer
Ayres	William	20		Bricklayer
Bailey	John	16		Shoemaker
Boulton	John	17		Labourer

Passenger Lists

Surname	First Name	Age		Occupation
Cameron	William	19		Labourer
Elmers	Henry	23		Agricultural Labourer
Finch	John	27		Labourer
Gibbs	James	33		Labourer
	Thomas	8		
Grauben	John	20		Agricultural Labourer
Hancock	Anthony	22		Labourer
Hepworth	George	26		Labourer
Jackson	Joseph	22		Farm Labourer
Kerr	John	39		Shepherd
Kimmersmants	Henry	26		Agricultural Labourer
Lens	Henry	20		Labourer
Ludiman	Henry	23		Agricultural Labourer
Luesen	Dedrick	22		Agricultural Labourer
Lutchens	Henry	23		Agricultural Labourer
	John	19		Agricultural Labourer
Monke	Frederick	23		Agricultural Labourer
Rose	Alexander	21		Labourer
Schaeffer	Hanry	23		Agricultural Labourer
Schwieters	Alexander	22		Agricultural Labourer
Shaw	George	26		Carter
Stokes	Thomas	24		Carpenter
Wagstaff	Henry	23		Carpenter
Wells	Edwin	14		Labourer
White	William	25		Labourer
Single Women				
Arthry	Hannah	20		Dairymaid
Atkins	Ellen	35		Nurse & General Servant
Bidley	Mary	26		General Servant
Boulton	Sarah	19		Nurse & General Servant
Brunning	Sarah D	41		Nurse
	Sarah A	22		House & Nursery Maid
Cameron	Ann	26		Servant
Elms	Matthea	18		General Servant
Gibbs	Elizabeth	18		General Servant
Jones	Susanna	22		Dairy & Family Servant
Franks	Helen	20		Ladies Maid
Ridley	Lucy	30		Dressmaker
Wells	Amelia	22		Laundress
	Rosetta	21		Laundress
	Miriam	2		
Wise	Elizabeth	22		Dressmaker

Cashmere Passengers 1857 to New Plymouth and Auckland

London (19 Dec 1856) to New Plymouth[132] (5 Apr 1857) and Auckland[43] (14 Apr 1857)

Under Captain George Pearson

Passengers listed at New Plymouth[132]	
Waller	Thomas
Waller	Mrs
Waller	Child
Penwarden	Thomas
Penwarden	Mrs
Penwarden	8 children
Jones	James
Jones	Wife
Jones	Child
Sands	William
Sands	Wife
Sands	Child
Perry	John
Perry	Wife
Perry	5 children
Scost	Emily
Tulford	Samuel
Wright	J.
Okey	T.
Passengers listed at Auckland[43]	
Adlain	Joshua
Barr	Thomas
Barr	Sarah
Bartlett	George
Bartlett	Eliza
Bartlett	Walter
Bartlett	Eliza
Bartlett	emma
Bartlett	Mary Ann
Binnick	Harriet
Clifford	Peter
Clifford	Mary
Clifford	John
Cook	John
Cook	Sarah
Cook	Eliza
Cook	Robert
Cook	Mary
Cook	William
Cook	Caroline
Cook	Emily
Cozens	Harriet
Cozens	Mary
Davidson	John
Davidson	Wiliam C.

Dickenson	John
Dixon	Mary A.
Dixon	Mark
Eustace	Alfred
Eustace	Hannah
Farmer	Miss.
Field	A.
Fleming	W.H.
Forsaith	Mr. T. S.
Forsaith	Mrs.
Forsaith	Miss
Goodfellow	Mr. John
Goodfellow	John, Jnr
Goodfellow	Euphemia
Guttred	Mary
Halnon	Joseph
Hawes	R.
Johnston	Mr. H. B.
Loing	Pauline
Lovelock	Elizabeth
Lovelock	Elizabeth
Lynds	William
Lynds	Louisa
Lynds	Louisa
Lynds	John
Lynds	Mary
Lynds	William A.
Lynds	Martha
Lynds	Philip
Marks	Patrick
Marks	Hannah
Marks	Ann
Marks	Stephen
Mccardle	Rose
Mcelwaine	Mr.
Mcelwaine	Mrs.
Mcelwaine	Richard
Mcelwaine	Walter R.
Mcintosh	Archibald
Mcintosh	Margaret
Mcintosh	Archibald
Mcintosh	Donald
Mcintosh	Nancy
Minns	James
Moore	Charles
Moore	Laura

Passenger Lists

Moore	Laura Fanny
Moore	Henry
Moore	Jane
Moore	Frank
Moore	Clara
Moore	Alexander
Moseley	A.H.
Okey	Edward
Okey	Ann
Okey	Mary
Okey	Edward
Okey	L. N.
Ricket	Caroline
Ricket	Jane
Ricket	Elizabeth
Ricket	J. W.
Ricket	Joseph
Ricket	Christopher
Roberts	Eliza
Rogers	J.

Savage	Ellen
Savage	James
Southgate	Emma
Street	Alfred
Thornton	James
Thornton	Ann
Thornton	Elizabeth
Thornton	Robert
Thornton	Edmund
Tuttey	William
Wallace	N. J.
Waller	Thomas
Waller	Mary
Waller	Thomas
Wilson	Mr. J. A.
Wilson	Mrs.
Wilson	Child
Yates	Henry L.

Cashmere Passengers 1859 to Lyttelton

London (11 Jun 1859) to Lyttelton (11 Oct 1859)

Under Captain Byron

Name		Age	County	Occupation
Chief cabin				
Bean	Mr and Mrs			
Chamier	Mr			
Chandler	Miss			
Compton	Miss			
Ellwell	Mr			
Fooks	Mr			
Fuller	Mr			
Hill	Miss			
Millson	Mr, Mrs and Miss			
Quaile	Mr			
Slayter	Mr			
Wave	Mr, Mrs and two children			
Willmott	Mr			
Second cabin				
Allen	Mr			
Baker	Mr and Mrs			
Collville	Mr			
Cooper	Mr			
De gaies	Mr			
Goldie	Mr			
Hayter	Mr			
Hewitt	Mr			
Hope	Mr			
Joynt	Mr and Mrs and two			

	children			
Joynt	Mr			
Kirkhouse	Mr			
Pepperill	Mr and Mrs and four children			
Rall	Mr			
Wilkinson	Mr			
Steerage				
Anderson	Mr J. and wife and one child			*Child (Elizabeth) died on board 1 October*
Bowls	R.			
Dean	H.			
Ellis	R.			
Guilbert	Henry			
Hanley	Frederick and wife, one child			
Martin	William - for Otago			
Offer	T.			
Families & children				
Atkinson	Robert	58	Durham	Joiner
	Isabella	38		*Died on board on 27 Sept*
	John D.	11		
	Robert	8		*Died on board on 27 July*
	Elizabeth	3		
	Charles W.	8 months		*Died on board on July*
Askew	Thomas	34	Middlesex	General labourer
	Ann	33		
	William	5		
Baker	William Simpson	47	Surrey	Plumber
	Sarah	47		
	John	18	T/F to single men	
Hill	John	41	Middlesex	Labourer - travelled with Baker
	Fanny	42		
	Anne	16	T/F single women	
	Margaret	11		
	Louisa	9		
	Fanny	7		
Sinclair	Fanny	22	T/F single women	Travelled with Baker
	William	21	T/F to single men	
Barrett	Robert	40	Glamorgan	Labourer
	Ann	33		
	William	9		
Capstaff	William	24	Durham	Shipwright
	Ann	22		
Clarke	Charles	31	Surrey	Farm labourer
	Anne	31		
Cox	William	26	Guernsey	Labourer
	Arabella	23		
	John	3 months		*Died on board on 2 July*

Passenger Lists

Craighead	John	44	Forfar	Ploughman
	Helen	44		
	John	14	T/F to single men	
	Alexander	11		
	Margaret	8		
	Thomas	5		
	David	2		
	Bruce	Infant		*Born & died on board on 6 July*
Davidson	Andrew	43	Northumberland	Labourer
	Elizabeth	33		
	George	4		*Died on board on 19 July*
	Arthur	1		
De la mare	Thomas	35	Mevagissy	Cooper - son-in-law to Thomas Glanville
	Mary	36		
	William Henry	7		
	Thomas Uriah	5		
	John Glanville	2		*Died on board on 26 June*
	Albert	6 months		*Died on board on 16 September*
Fraser	James	25	Aberdeen	Farm servant
	Jean	25		
	Daughter			*Born on board on 14 September*
Glanville	Thomas	60	Mevagissy	Labourer
	Mary	61		
	Jane	31	T/F single women	
	Caroline	23	T/F single women	
Graves	James	31	Wicklow	Labourer
	Mary Ann	26		
	Catherine	7		
	James	1		*Died on board on 28 July*
Gray	James	33	Yorkshire	Farm labourer
	Martha	33		
	Ann	3		*Died on board on 1 July, name was noted as Emma?*
	Alice	1 month		
Gunn	John	26	Caithness	Shepherd
	Isabella	20		
	David	1		
Ingerfield	Charles	23	Hampshire	Labourer
	Matilda	20		
King	Joseph or Josiah	26	Durham	Smith
	Jane	26		*Died on board on 21 July*
	Margaret Jane	1½		*Died on board on 7 July*
	Daughter, Jane Lack			*Born on board 14 July and died 24 July*
King	John	36	Durham	Iron moulder

	Amelia	38			
	John	10			
	Robert	8			
	Amelia	6			
Lord	Thomas	27	Inverness	Farm labourer	
	Ann	24			
	Elias	3			
	Fedo	4 mths			
Luffy	Thomas	26	Galway	Farm labourer	
	Bridget	24			
	Mary	2			
Munro	Donald	22	Ross	Farm labourer	
	Isbella	28			
	Son			**Born on board on 3 October**	
Richardson	James	35	Durham	Cartwright	
	Ann	34			
Richardson	William	34	Somersetshire	Shepherd	
	Harriet	29			
Roskrage	James	46	Cornwall	Farm labourer	
	Elizabeth	38			
	Ann	15	T/F single women		
	Thomas	13	T/F to single men		
	Lucy	11			
	Julia	9			
	Marie	7			
	Richard	5			
Shaney	William	23	Wiltshire	Labourer	
	Louisa	24			
Silvester	John	36	Nottinghamshire	Labourer	
	Maria	30		*Mrs Maria Silvester and the youngest child were taken out of the ship at Gravesend the child having whooping cough.*	
	George	8			
	Sarah	4			
	Fanny	1¾			
Tweedy	Stephen	46			
	Ann	45			
	Ann	20	T/F single women		
	Deborah	17	T/F single women		
	Dorothy	13	T/F single women		
	Eleanor	10			
	Joseph	8			
	Sarah	5			
Willson	John	44	Durham	Potter	
	Dorothy	42			
	John	12	T/F to single men		
	Ralph	9			
	William	7			
	Joseph	5			
	Isaac	5			
	Henry	3			

McKaile	Wentworth			Adult & child boarded in place of Mrs Silvester & child.
	Child			
Single men				
Anderson	Thomas	16	Dumfries	Farm labourer
Baker	John	18	Kent	Carpenter
Craighead	John	14		Farm labourer
Dorley	Thomas	22	Galway	Farm labourer
Elder	Peter	23	Caithness	Shepherd
Glendinning	George	35	Edinburgh	Shepherd
Hughan	John	42	Dumfries	Shepherd
	Joan	18	T/F single women	
	Janet	16	T/F single women	
	Thomas	13		
	John	11		
	Jane	10	T/F single women	
	Isabella	7	T/F single women	
	Margaret	5	T/F single women	
Mcilwrick	James	21	Wigtown	Shepherd
Mclean	Alexander	22	Perth	Shepherd
Pearce	William	28	Surrey	Barristers clerk
Pearson	William	20	Nottinghamshire	Labourer
Roskrage	Thomas	13	Cornwall	Farm labourer
Ross	Thomas	21	Ross	Shepherd
Shayler	William	11		
Silvester	Henry	22	Nottinghamshire	Farm labourer
Sinclair	William	21		Bricklayer
Spring	Charles	19	Middlesex	Watchouseman
Steel	John	16	Durham	Shipwright
Willson	John	12	Durham	Potter
Single women				
Fletcher	Mary Ann	38	Surrey	Dressmaker – Matron on ship
Granville	Jane	31		Domestic servant
	Caroline	23		Domestic servant
Hayward	Ann	24	Kent	Domestic servant
Hill	Anne	16		Domestic servant
Hughan	Joan	18	Dumfries	Domestic servant
	Janet	16	Dumfries	Domestic servant
	Jane	10	Dumfries	
	Isabella	7	Dumfries	
	Mary	5	Dumfries	
Mitchell	Mary R.	18	Forfar	Domestic servant
Roskrage	Ann	15	Cornwall	Domestic servant
Shayler	Annie	21	Surrey	Domestic servant
	William	11	T/F to single men	
Sinclair	Fanny	22	Middlesex	Dom serv. **Died on board 7 August**
Tempany	Marion	24	Surrey	Dressmaker
Tweedy	Ann	20		Domestic servant
	Deborah	17		Domestic servant
	Dorothy	13		Domestic servant

Cashmere Passengers 1861 to Port Chalmers and Lyttelton[58]

London (21Nov 1860) to Port Chalmers (9 Feb 1861) and Lyttelton (15 Feb 1861)

Under Captain Petherbridge

Otago Passengers	
Wilkinson	Thomas Merrett (ship's surgeon)
2 dogs	
6 horses	
5 rams	
Hadcock?	Mr. R. V.
Jones	Mr. Jas.
Inverarity	Mr. D.
Boland	Mr. T. D.
Richardson	Mr. G. P.
Wells	Miss
Boland	Misses (3)
Spooner	Mrs.

Chch Passengers[58]	
Chief Cabin	
Spooner	Mrs and three children
Haskins	Mr. T. G.
Reddick	Miss A.
Steerage	
Gillatt	Jos.
Gillatt	Wife of Jos.
Bristow	R.
Pearson	W.
Pearson	J.
Cholmondely	T.
Grint	J. F.
Neeve	A.
Clarke	G.
Grint	Charlotte

Cashmere Passengers 1862 to Auckland[62]

London (15 Dec 1861) to Auckland (7 Apr 1862)

Under Captain Petherbridge

Banbury	Edwin
Banbury	John
Baylis	Susan
Bleakley	Eliza
Bolton	Charles
Bolton	William
Carr	Ann
Carr	James
Carr	Thomas
Clark	John F.
Cooper	Charles F.
Cooper	Mrs Charlotte
Cottingham	Lewis
Dean	Clara
Dean	Florence
Dooley	Johauna
Dooley	Mary
Dora	Miss

East	James
Edward	William
Ford	Emily
Ford	William
Fraser	Alexander
Hicks	Mary Jane
Holmes	Annie
Holmes	Ellen
Holmes	Emily
Holmes	Helen
Holmes	James H.
Holmes	John H.
Holmes	Julia
Holmes	Mary
Horace	J.T.
Horace	Mrs
Jones	Clement
Lumsden	Andrew
Lyons	C.

Maugham	Elizabeth		Redshaw	John
Maugham	H.R.		Redshaw	Joseph
Maugham	Mrs Sarah		Redshaw	Mary
Maugham	Thomas		Sayer	Alfred
Maugham	William		Shannon	Ann
Mclaughlin	Andrew		Shannon	D.
Milbourne	Annie M.		Stewart	Catherine
Milbourne	Eliza		Stewart	Nathaniel
Milbourne	Eliza R.		Streeter	Mary
Milbourne	Fanny E.		Vidul	George
Milbourne	Frances		Vidul	Selwyn
Miller	Amelia Ann		Walton/Walten	Maria
			Whyte	Elizabeth
Miller	Amelia Ann		Whyte	James
			Wilks	Mary M.
Miller	William J.		Wilson	J.J.
Miller	William J.		Wood	Dr John
Nihil	Infant		Wood	Mrs
Nihil	Mrs W.		Worms	Mrs
Redshaw	Alice		Worms	Samuel
Redshaw	Emma			

Cashmere Passengers 1863 to Nelson[67]

London (3 Jul 1863) to Nelson (14 Oct 1863)

Under Captain Barnett

Cabin Passengers			Sladden	Elizabeth Jane
Beale	Benjamin S.		Sladden	Emily
Brabant	Henry		Sladden	Jemima
Burrell	Miss E.		Sladden	Mary
Burrell	Miss M.		Sladden	Matilda
O'Brien	Alexander		Sladden	Mr and Mrs
Steerage			Sladden	Sarah Anne
Ainsworth	John		Stewart	Jessie
Bird	Susan		Stewart	Mary Ann
Botham	Eleanor		Watson	Robert
Botham	Mr and Mrs.		Webster	Mr And Mrs
Keeby	John		Williams	Charles
Kendrick	John		Williams	Mary
Lynch	Emma		Williams	Mr And Mrs
Mccullum	Robert		Williams	Nancy
Sladden	Caroline		Williams	Rebecca
Sladden	Charlotte		Williams	Thomas
Sladden	Eliza			

References

1. ShipsCar-Cey. at <http://users.xplornet.com/~shipping/ShipsC1.htm>
2. What is a Clipper Ship? | Marine Insight. at <http://www.marineinsight.com/marine/life-at-sea/maritime-history/what-is-a-clipper-ship-2/>
3. John Cracroft Wilson. *Wikipedia, the free encyclopedia* (2013). at <http://en.wikipedia.org/w/index.php?title=John_Cracroft_Wilson&oldid=580697034>
4. In Memoriam. Captain George Pearson. 11 April 1892. *Auckland Star* 4 (1892).
5. The Countess Of Kintore | NZETC. at <http://nzetc.victoria.ac.nz/tm/scholarly/tei-Bre01Whit-t1-body-d96.html>
6. Papers Past — North Otago Times — 28 March 1877 — CHRISTCHURCH. March 27. at <http://paperspast.natlib.govt.nz/cgi-bin/paperspast?a=d&cl=search&d=NOT18770328.2.9.4&srpos=4&e=-------100--1--on--0%22captain+petherbridge%22-->
7. Page 1 Advertisements Column 1. Captain Barnett late of the Cresswell. 24 November 1863. *Colonist* 1 (1863).
8. Wikipedia contributors. Packet ship. *Wikipedia, the free encyclopedia* (2012). at <http://en.wikipedia.org/w/index.php?title=Packet_ship&oldid=481049374>
9. Shipping lines involved in New Zealand immigration. at <http://freepages.genealogy.rootsweb.ancestry.com/~nzbound/lines.htm#Willis,%20Gann%20and%20Co.>
10. Haws, Duncan. Shaw, Savill & Albion. at <http://www.merchantnavyofficers.com/shawsavill.html>
11. Taonga, N. Z. M. for C. and H. T. M. Settlement in the provinces: 1853 to 1870. at <http://www.teara.govt.nz/en/history-of-immigration/5>
12. Shaw, Savill And Albion Company | NZETC. at <http://nzetc.victoria.ac.nz/tm/scholarly/tei-Bre01Whit-t1-body-d5.html>
13. Costs and Wages in Great Britain. at <http://www.rootsweb.ancestry.com/~irlcar2/wages.htm>
14. Purdy, F. On the Earnings of Agricultural Labourers in England and Wales, 1860. *Journal of the Statistical Society of London* **24,** 328–373 (1861).
15. William Kirk Papers, MS-Papers-7207-01-PLAN, Alexander Turnbull Library, Wellington, New Zealand. 1854.
16. Life at Sea: Museum Victoria. at <http://museumvictoria.com.au/discoverycentre/websites-mini/journeys-australia/1850s70s/life-at-sea/>
17. Diver, M. *The Voyages of the Clontarf.* (Dornie Publishing Company, 2011).
18. Glasgow Herald (Glasgow, Scotland), Thursday, October 21, 1869; Issue 9298.
19. Albin Martin Diary Ref # ARC 1900.39, Canterbury Museum.
20. Shipping List. 1851 voyage of the *Cashmere* with summary and cabin passengers. 21 October 1851. *Daily Southern Cross* 2 (1851).
21. Vessels In Harbour. The *Cashmere* journey 1853 to Auckland. Journey Summary. 10 May 1853. *Daily Southern Cross* 2 (1853).
22. Delay in the channel. The Morning Post (London, England), Monday, November 29, 1852; pg. 3; Issue 24629. 19th Century British Library Newspapers: Part II.
23. Naval Intelligence.. The Times (London, England), Monday, Nov 29, 1852; pg. 7; Issue 21285.
24. Chapter XVI.... | NZETC. Through Ninety Years, 1826-1916: Life and Work Among the Maoris in New Zealand. Notes of the Lives of William and William Leonard Williams, First and Third Bishops of Waiapu. at <http://nzetc.victoria.ac.nz/tm/scholarly/tei-WilThro-t1-body-d16.html>
25. The Recent Hurricane.. The Times (London, England), Wednesday, Dec 29, 1852; pg. 8; Issue 21311.
26. Shipping Intelligence. *Cashmere* from Auckland to New Plymouth. 13 July 1853. *Taranaki Herald* 2 (1853).
27. Shipping List. George Pearson testimonial. 24 June 1853. *Daily Southern Cross* 2 (1853).
28. Coral Sea Islands. *Wikipedia, the free encyclopedia* (2014). at

<http://en.wikipedia.org/w/index.php?title=Coral_Sea_Islands&oldid=563078960>
29. Willis Island (Coral Sea). *Wikipedia, the free encyclopedia* (2014). at <http://en.wikipedia.org/w/index.php?title=Willis_Island_(Coral_Sea)&oldid=590033684>
30. Discovery of new Islands in the Torres Strait. The Morning Chronicle (London, England), Thursday, November 17, 1853; Issue 27114.
31. Coordinates of the *Cashmere*. The Morning Post (London, England), Saturday, July 22, 1854; pg. 8; Issue 25133. 19th Century British Library Newspapers: Part II.
32. Shipping Intelligence. 1854 voyage summary for *Cashmere*. 23 August 1854. *Wellington Independent* 3 (1854).
33. Journal of Revd. John Macky. Dates covered: 1854-1863. Reference number: MNP MS 134. South Auckland Research Centre, Auckland, New Zealand.
34. The Macky Family in New Zealand · The Journal of Reverend John Macky · Commencing 10 April 1854. at <http://macky.net/journal.html>
35. The Lyttelton Times. News of the Crimean War. 25 October 1855. *Lyttelton Times* 4 (1855).
36. Captain Parsons (Harbour) to Superintendent - passenger list of *Cashmere*. Filed 1081(1) - 12/11/1855 (R22185055) Archives New Zealand, Christchurch Office.
37. Harman (Emigration) to Provincial Secretary - sailings per *Cashmere* - 2/10/1855 (R22184994). Archives New Zealand, Christchurch Office.
38. Harman (Emigration) to Superintendent - *Cashmere* sailing with 156 souls - 26/10/1855 (R22185035). Archives New Zealand, Christchurch Office.
39. Shipping News. Passengers for New Plymouth. 17 November 1855. *Lyttelton Times* 7 (1855).
40. Shipping Intelligence. *Cashmere* for China. 28 November 1855. *Taranaki Herald* 3 (1855).
41. Papers Past — Daily Southern Cross — 14 December 1855 — Port of Auckland. SHIPPING INTELLIGENCE. at <http://paperspast.natlib.govt.nz/cgi-bin/paperspast?a=d&cl=search&d=DSC18551214.2.3&srpos=132&e=22-10-1855-31-12-1855--100--101-byDA-on--0*Cashmere*-->
42. Hawkins, D N (1983). *Rangiora: the passing years and people in a Canterbury country town.* Rangiora: Rangiora Borough Council.
43. Papers Past — Daily Southern Cross — 17 April 1857 — Shipping Intelligence. PORT OF AUCKLAND. at <http://paperspast.natlib.govt.nz/cgi-bin/paperspast?a=d&cl=search&d=DSC18570417.2.3&srpos=19&e=01-04-1857-31-04-1857--100--1--on--0*Cashmere*-->
44. Arrivals. Some passengers on 1857 *Cashmere* voyage. 17 April 1857. *Daily Southern Cross* 3 (1857).
45. Fitzgerald (Emigration) to Superintendent - books per the *Cashmere* - 11/10/1859 (R22188376). Archives New Zealand. Christchurch Office.
46. Shipping News. 1859 arrival of the *Cashmere* with journey summary and passenger list. 12 October 1859. *Lyttelton Times* 4 (1859).
47. Resident Magistrate's Court, Lyttelton. Young boy dies on *Cashmere*. 15 October 1859. *Lyttelton Times* 5 (1859).
48. Shipping News. 1859 Testimonials. 15 October 1859. *Lyttelton Times* 4 (1859).
49. Donald, Latter and Luck (Immigration Commissioners) to Provincial Secretary - report '*Cashmere*' - 24/12/1858 (R22187804). Archives New Zealand, Christchurch Office.
50. Resident Magistrates' Court. James Pearson charged with assault. 29 October 1859. *Lyttelton Times* 5 (1859).
51. Doctor Donald (Immigration) to Provincial Secretary - reports on patients from the *Cashmere* at Immigration barracks, Lyttelton - 4/11/1859 (R22188470). Archives New Zealand. Christchurch Office.
52. Years Fitzgerald (Emigration) to Superintendent - telegraph goods per '*Cashmere*' - 22/09/1859 (R22188297). Archives New Zealand. Christchurch Office.
53. Fitzgerald (Emigration) to Superintendent - '*Cashmere*' - 26/08/1859 [3 items separated from this file as SEP Nos 680a, 680c, 680n] (R22188292). Archives New Zealand. Christchurch Office.
54. J.E. Fitzgerald (Emigration) to Superintendent - cases per *Cashmere* - 7/03/1860 (R22188792). Archives New Zealand. Christchurch Office.
55. Local Intelligence. Loading wool on the *Cashmere*. 14 December 1859. *Lyttelton Times* 4 (1859).
56. Local Intelligence. *Cashmere* fires its guns. 17 December 1859. *Lyttelton Times* 4 (1859).

57. Departure of the *Cashmere*. 14 March 1860. *Lyttelton Times* 4 (1860).
58. Shipping News. 1861 voyage on *Cashmere* and passengers. 16 February 1861. *Lyttelton Times* 4 (1861).
59. Local Intelligence. 1861 voyage, horses died. 20 February 1861. *Lyttelton Times* 4 (1861).
60. Shipping News. 1861 arrival at Otago. 9 February 1861. *Otago Witness* 4 5 (1861).
61. Shipping Intelligence. Arrival of the *Cashmere*. 22 February 1861. *Wellington Independent* 2 (1861).
62. Port Of Onehunga. 1862 arrival of the *Cashmere*. 8 April 1862. *Daily Southern Cross* 5 (1862).
63. Wilson, J. J. Wilson, John James, 1840-1918 : Journal of a voyage on the *Cashmere* / transcribed by Marsha Donaldson. (1861). at <http://natlib.govt.nz/records/23192070>
64. VESSELS SPOKEN. The Sydney Morning Herald. 19 April 1862. *The Sydney Morning Herald* 8 (1862).
65. Shipping. 1862 arrival of the *Cashmere*. 18 April 1862. *Colonist* 2 (1862).
66. Pakeha's Birds. The arrival of birds on the *Cashmere*. 23 September 1926. *Auckland Star* 16 (1926).
67. Shipping Intelligence. 1863 arrival of the *Cashmere* into Nelson. Journey summary. 15 October 1863. *Nelson Examiner and New Zealand Chronicle* 2 (1863).
68. The Colonist. Nelson, Friday, October 16, 1863. The Landmarks Of Party In New Zealand. *Colonist* 2 3 (1863).
69. Local Intelligence. Resident Magistrate's Court. Desertions. 17 December 1863. *Nelson Examiner and New Zealand Chronicle* 2 (1863).
70. Expected Arrivals. *Cashmere* from Nelson for New Plymouth. Man lost overboard. 17 December 1863. *Wellington Independent* 2 (1863).
71. Bowle makes an escape. 1 January 1864. *Colonist* 2 (1864).
72. Accidental Death Of Mr. Bloor, Late Surgeon Of The *Cashmere*. 19 January 1864. *Colonist* 2 (1864).
73. Blunders In The Government Statistics. Wool on the *Cashmere*. 12 September 1864. *Nelson Examiner and New Zealand Chronicle* 5 (1864).
74. Customs Entries. Inwards. The *Cashmere* loads with wool at Nelson. 9 March 1864. *Otago Daily Times* 4 (1864).
75. Call Of Death. Mr. John Banbury. 14 May 1936. *Auckland Star* 17 (1936).
76. Farmers | NZETC. Thomas Bolton. at <http://nzetc.victoria.ac.nz//tm/scholarly/tei-Cyc03Cycl-t1-body1-d6-d29-d2.html>
77. Obituary. Mr. H. S. Brabant. 5 May 1926. *Auckland Star* 11 (1926).
78. Obituary. Mrs Elizabeth Alice Bray. 25 June 1925. *Auckland Star* 10 (1925).
79. Mr R. Bristow. 9 May 1914. *Press* 16 (1914).
80. Miss Elizabeth Jane Compton. 1 March 1904. *Ashburton Guardian* 3 (1904).
81. Obituary. William Cowie. 7 July 1945. *Auckland Star* 6 (1945).
82. Obituary. Arabella Cox. 15 March 1899. *Press* 6 (1899).
83. Old Colonists | NZETC. John Craighead. at <http://nzetc.victoria.ac.nz//tm/scholarly/tei-Cyc03Cycl-t1-body1-d6-d42-d3.html>
84. Farmers | NZETC. David Craighead. at <http://nzetc.victoria.ac.nz//tm/scholarly/tei-Cyc03Cycl-t1-body1-d6-d42-d2.html>
85. Mr Peter Elder. 25 October 1913. *Press* 13 (1913).
86. Obituary. Mr. Alfred Eustace. 18 August 1920. *New Zealand Herald* 8 (1920).
87. Local And General News. Mr John Ferguson. 30 November 1901. *New Zealand Herald* 4 5 (1901).
88. Obituary. Mrs Samuel Fleming. 28 March 1913. *Auckland Star* 5 (1913).
89. Women In Print. Mrs Amelia Ann Foster. 5 October 1925. *Evening Post* 13 (1925).
90. Farmers | NZETC. Joseph Robinson Gilliatt. at <http://nzetc.victoria.ac.nz//tm/scholarly/tei-Cyc03Cycl-t1-body1-d6-d102-d2.html>
91. Mr. James Gray,... | NZETC. at <http://nzetc.victoria.ac.nz//tm/scholarly/tei-Cyc03Cycl-t1-body1-d4-d4-d19.html>
92. Farmers | NZETC. David Gunn. at <http://nzetc.victoria.ac.nz//tm/scholarly/tei-Cyc03Cycl-t1-body1-d7-d19-d2.html>
93. Deaths Of Old Colonists. Mrs R. Hall. 9 May 1916,. *New Zealand Herald* 9 (1916).
94. The Rev. Thomas Hamer. 21 June 1899. *Auckland Star* 2 (1899).

95. Personal Matters. Mr. Lewis Alexander Hamerton. 21 August 1914. *Evening Post* 2 (1914).
96. Personal. Mr Thomas Edward Hamerton. 23 July 1919. *Wanganui Chronicle* 4 (1919).
97. Part III. PART III. Biographical Sketches... | NZETC. Captain Robert Chisenhall Hamerton. at <http://nzetc.victoria.ac.nz//tm/scholarly/tei-WarEarl-t1-body-d20.html>
98. Mrs F. G. Hawley. 23 July 1912. *Press* 7 (1912).
99. The Thames Star. Resurrexi. Wednesday, March 6, 1895. Mrs D. Henderson. 6 March 1895. *Thames Star* 2 (1895).
100. Sudden Death At Thames. Mrs David Henderson. 7 March 1895. *New Zealand Herald* 5 (1895).
101. Page 3 Advertisements Column 2. Mrs Heyward Obituary. 21 December 1897. *Star* 3 (1897).
102. Death Of Mr. Shirley Hill. 27 August 1908. *New Zealand Herald* 6 (1908).
103. Obituary. William Emms Ivory. 26 April 1911. *Press* 10 (1911).
104. Obituary. Mr Joseph Jackson. 6 March 1909. *Press* 10 (1909).
105. Ex-Mayors | NZETC. Moss Jonas. at <http://nzetc.victoria.ac.nz//tm/scholarly/tei-Cyc03Cycl-t1-body1-d7-d1-d3.html>
106. Mr Moss Jonas. 6 November 1907. *Press* 8 (1907).
107. Junior University Scholarships. Mr William Lynds. 27 January 1902. *Auckland Star* 4 (1902).
108. Taonga, N. Z. M. for C. and H. T. M. Martin, Albin. at <http://www.teara.govt.nz/en/biographies/2m34/martin-albin>
109. Local And General News. Mrs McCall. 11 November 1899. *New Zealand Herald* 5 (1899).
110. Obituary. Mr William R. McCall. 11 October 1937. *Auckland Star* 3 (1937).
111. Personal. Mr Edward Okey. 31 January 1910. *Manawatu Standard* 5 (1910).
112. Great Grandma's Wicker Basket: The Pearce Family. at <http://greatgrandmaswickerbasket.blogspot.co.nz/2012/05/pearce-family.html>
113. Farmers | NZETC. William Pearson. at <http://nzetc.victoria.ac.nz//tm/scholarly/tei-Cyc03Cycl-t1-body1-d6-d6-d2.html>
114. Obituary. Henry Horsford Prins. 9 November 1896. *Star* 2 (1896).
115. Obituary. Mr. Joseph Rickit. 6 April 1926. *Auckland Star* 3 (1926).
116. Obituary. Mrs D. H. Rutherford. 2 December 1910. *Manawatu Standard* 5 (1910).
117. Mrs Elizabeth Runciman. 5 September 1887. *Auckland Star* 4 (1887).
118. News Of The Day. Mrs F. Schmidt. 5 February 1900. *Press* 4 5 (1900).
119. Ex-Councillors... | NZETC. Walter Henry Scott. at <http://nzetc.victoria.ac.nz/tm/scholarly/tei-Cyc06Cycl-t1-body1-d1-d7.html>
120. Rangiora. Mr Joseph Stanton. 2 October 1913. *Press* 10 (1913).
121. Mrs Hannah Stapleforth. 28 March 1907. *Auckland Star* 4 (1907).
122. Mrs. William Stichbury. 28 January 1938. *Auckland Star* 3 (1938).
123. Local And General News. Thomas Warner. 25 July 1899. *New Zealand Herald* 5 (1899).
124. Farmers | NZETC. George Watson and William Morgan Watson. at <http://nzetc.victoria.ac.nz//tm/scholarly/tei-Cyc03Cycl-t1-body1-d6-d24-d2.html#Cyc03Cycl-fig-Cyc03Cycl0726b>
125. Long – Lived Family. Wells family. 2 August 1924. *New Zealand Herald* 8 (1924).
126. Obituary. Mr. James Wells. 9 August 1938. *Evening Post* 13 (1938).
127. Mr. Thomas Merrett Wilkinson | NZETC. at <http://nzetc.victoria.ac.nz/tm/scholarly/tei-Cyc04Cycl-t1-body1-d2-d10-d18.html>
128. Obituary. Mr. John Alexander Wilson. 30 November 1928. *Evening Post* 11 (1928).
129. Old Identity's Death. Mr John James Wilson. 25 April 1918. *New Zealand Herald* 8 (1918).
130. Port Of Auckland. 1854 *Cashmere* passenger list. 22 August 1854. *Daily Southern Cross* 2 (1854).
131. New Zealand, Archives New Zealand, Passenger Lists, 1839-1973 Image New Zealand, Archives New Zealand, Passenger Lists, 1839-1973; pal:/MM9.3.1/TH-266-11563-20900-68 — FamilySearch.org. at <https://familysearch.org/pal:/MM9.3.1/TH-266-11563-20900-68?cc=1609792&wc=MP7J-KFC:119115301,119046202,119115302>
132. Papers Past — Taranaki Herald — 11 April 1857 — Shipping Intelligence. at <http://paperspast.natlib.govt.nz/cgi-bin/paperspast?a=d&cl=search&d=TH18570411.2.3&srpos=2&e=--1857---1857--100--1--on--0*Cashmere*-ARTICLE->

www.ingramcontent.com/pod-product-compliance
Lightning Source LLC
Chambersburg PA
CBHW050648160426
43194CB00010B/1855